Tests of
General Educational
Development

Administrator's Guide

Official GED Practice Tests

Includes:
- **Answer Explanations (Rationales) for Each Test Question**
- Answer Keys
- Conversion Tables
- Recommended Prescriptions for Additional Study

GED Testing Service™
American Council on Education

 Tests of General Educational Development

Developed by the GED Testing Service
One Dupont Circle NW, Suite 250
Washington, D.C. 20036
www.gedtest.org

Full-Length Test Form
Administrator's Guide
Official GED® Practice Test for the 2002 Series GED® Tests

Steck-Vaughn is the exclusive distributor of the Official GED® Practice Tests

An Imprint of HMH
Supplemental Publishers

www.SteckVaughn.com/GED
800-531-5015

Full-Length Test Form Administrator's Guide ISBNs:
ISBN-13: 978-1-4190-5382-5
ISBN-10: 1-4190-5382-5

Full-Length Test Form/Official GED Complete Package ISBNs:
ISBN-13: 978-1-4190-5375-7
ISBN-10: 1-4190-5375-2

Full-Length Test Form/Five sets of the full battery of test booklets ISBNs:
ISBN-13: 978-1-4190-5388-7
ISBN-10: 1-4190-5388-4

Copyright © 2008, American Council on Education

No part of this publication may be reproduced, stored in a retrieval system, or transmitted in any form or by any means without the prior written permission of the American Council on Education.

Printed in the United States of America
2 3 4 5 6 7 8   0928   10

TABLE OF CONTENTS

Official GED Practice Tests Administrator's Guide: Full-Length Test Form

Overview 4
    The General Educational Development (GED) Testing Program 4
    Description of the Official GED Practice Tests: Full-Length Test Form 5
    How to Use the Official GED Practice Tests 7
    Analyzing and Interpreting Results of Official GED Practice Tests 9
    Questions and Answers About the Official GED Practice Tests 11

U.S. English Full-Length Test Form: Conversion Tables 12
    Language Arts, Writing 12
    Language Arts, Reading 14
    Social Studies 14
    Science 15
    Mathematics 15

U.S. English Full-Length Test Form: Answer Key 16
    Language Arts, Writing (also see Writing, Topic E on page 63) 16
    Language Arts, Reading 16
    Social Studies 16
    Science 16
    Mathematics 17

U.S. English Full-Length Test Form: Answer Explanations (Rationales) for Each Test Question 19
    Language Arts, Writing 19
    Language Arts, Reading 27
    Social Studies 37
    Science 49
    Mathematics 59

U.S. English Full-Length Test Form: Writing, Topic E 63
    Essay Directions 63
    Scoring the Essay 65

Steck-Vaughn Recommended Prescriptions for Additional Study 67
    Language Arts, Writing 67
    Language Arts, Reading 68
    Social Studies 70
    Science 71
    Mathematics 72

The General Educational Development (GED) Testing Program

Purpose of the GED Testing Program

The GED Tests began as a way for servicemen and servicewomen returning from World War II to demonstrate that they had the knowledge and skills necessary for employment and higher education. Since its beginning in 1942, the GED Testing Program has grown and evolved. There have been three previous generations of the GED Tests: 1942, 1978, and 1988. Changes made were the result of the identification of specific areas of need or assessment that would strengthen the tests and ensure its validity and credibility in a changing world.

Many adults have not completed a regular high school program of instruction. However, this fact does not mean that their educational growth and experiences ceased upon leaving school. People continue to learn through a variety of experiences encountered in everyday life. The purpose of the General Educational Development (GED) Testing Program is to provide a means by which learning acquired from such educational experiences can be evaluated and recognized. The GED Tests make it possible for qualified individuals to earn a high school credential, thus providing opportunities for hundreds of thousands of adults to:

- Pursue higher education
- Obtain specific jobs
- Gain promotions
- Achieve personal goals

Content of the GED Tests

The GED Tests are designed to measure the major and lasting outcomes and skills associated with four years of regular high school study. Five GED Tests cover the following major subject areas: Language Arts, Writing; Language Arts, Reading; Social Studies; Science; and Mathematics. Multiple-choice questions are used for each of the five test areas, with the following exceptions:

- *Part II* of the *Language Arts, Writing Test,* which requires the candidate to write an expository essay; and
- Twenty percent (20%) of the problems on *Parts I and II* of the *Mathematics Test,* which requires candidates to generate a numerical answer to alternate format questions and use a grid to record their responses.

Candidates are assessed on their knowledge of broad concepts as well as their ability to use knowledge, information, and skills to solve problems. The GED Tests include questions that assess candidates' abilities to apply, analyze, synthesize, and evaluate information. Interpreting visual text is an important aspect of the GED Tests. This new generation of GED Tests uses color to enhance the clarity and readability of graphics that are incorporated into the tests.

The 2002 Series GED Tests have been revised to ensure that the skills measured represent those found in a typical high school curriculum. To ensure that the GED Tests are aligned with current high school standards, the GEDTS conducted an extensive review of state and national academic standards. From this review, the GEDTS identified the knowledge and skills that graduating seniors actually have and can perform, not what they *should know* and *do*. It is this emphasis on performance that distinguishes the GED Tests from other assessment instruments. For more information on the GEDTS review of standards, see *Alignment of National and State Standards: A Report by the GED Testing Service* (American Council on Education, GEDTS, 1999).

Basis for GED High School Equivalency

GEDTS ensures through two basic methods that the tests are equivalent and can measure the knowledge and skills normally attained during a four-year program of study. The first is the identification of the content that is representative of the secondary school. The second is the evaluation of candidate performance based on a nationally representative sample of graduating high school seniors.

The content for the 2002 Series GED Tests resulted from an extensive review of state and national standards, including current high school curriculum content. Many people were involved in the identification of the content specifications, including teachers, curriculum specialists, and content experts. After the content areas were defined, test questions were developed and subjected to a rigorous review. In addition to the review, the questions were also pre-tested and revised before the final test forms were compiled.

The next part of the process was to establish the GED passing score. Approximately 10,000 graduating high school seniors participated in the norming process for the 2002 Series GED Tests. By testing graduating high school seniors, the GEDTS ensured that the knowledge and skills represented by the traditional diploma and the GED high school credential were comparable. The passing standard for the 2002 Series GED Tests, as in previous generations of the tests, has been set higher than that for graduation from high school. Approximately 42% of graduating high school seniors would be unable to pass the GED Tests.

For more information, visit www.gedtest.org.

Description of the Official GED Practice Tests: Full-Length Test Form

Purpose of the Official GED Practice Tests

The Official GED Practice Tests are designed to evaluate a candidate's readiness to take the actual full-length GED Tests. The Official GED Practice Tests include the same number of questions found on the GED Tests. All Official GED Practice Tests are developed based on the same specifications as the full-length tests, including a sample of questions that cover the same knowledge and skills. Questions included on the Official GED Practice Tests undergo the same rigorous review and norming with graduating high school seniors as do the questions on the full-length GED Tests.

Scores on the Official GED Practice Tests are based on the same standard score scale that is used by the GED Tests. This use of the same standard score scale ensures that the official GED Practice Tests are the only accurate predictions of how well a candidate is likely to do on the GED Tests.

In addition to predicting scores, the Official GED Practice Tests help instructors identify candidates' general areas of strength and weakness. However, these tests were not designed as diagnostic or prescriptive tools.

Finally, the Official GED Practice Tests provide candidates with experience in taking standardized tests. The Official GED Practice Tests enable the candidate to experience the types of questions that are on the GED Tests.

Number of Questions and Time Limits

The Official GED Practice Tests: Full-Length Test Form includes five subject area tests. The information below shows the number of questions and the recommended time limit for each test.

Language Arts, Writing
  Part I—50 multiple-choice questions; 75 minutes
  Part II—1 candidate-generated essay; 45 minutes

Language Arts, Reading
  40 multiple-choice questions; 65 minutes

Social Studies
  50 multiple-choice questions; 70 minutes

Science
  50 multiple-choice questions; 80 minutes

Mathematics
  Part I—26 multiple-choice and grid questions; 46 minutes
  Part II—24 multiple-choice and grid questions; 44 minutes

The Official GED Practice Tests must be administered using the time limits indicated above. If these time limits are not enforced, the resulting scores CANNOT predict the candidate's scores on the GED Tests. Helping candidates understand how to manage their time while in a timed-testing situation is an excellent test-taking strategy.

Skills Measured by the Tests

The GED Tests are organized into five subject areas:
- *Language Arts, Writing*
- *Language Arts, Reading*
- *Social Studies*
- *Science*
- *Mathematics*

In addition to the content-specific questions, the 2002 Series GED Tests assess skills across subject areas. For example, reading comprehension and processing information are two skills that a candidate must master in order to do well in all subjects and earn a GED high school credential.

The GED Tests require students to demonstrate their critical thinking and problem-solving skills. Higher order thinking skills are necessary when examinees are asked to:
- Apply concepts and principles
- Analyze relationships
- Synthesize information and ideas
- Evaluate the validity of information provided

Processing visual text is another important skill assessed on the GED Tests. Approximately 50% of the questions on the *Social Studies, Science,* and *Mathematics Tests* include interpreting information from visual text, such as charts, maps, graphs, and diagrams. Candidates must be able to interpret visual text and respond to related questions.

Readability

Questions used in the GED Tests are written or selected by practitioners—teachers and content experts current in the academic discipline represented.

The questions are then screened through a process of review by at least three independent teachers and content experts, and the GED test specialist who is a professional educator certified in that discipline. In this review, it is determined if the level of difficulty of the reading selections is appropriate for a high school graduate. Thus, the "readability" of the questions on all of the GED Tests is monitored early in the test development process through the judgment of experienced educators.

After questions have survived the first stage of screening, they are field-tested through administration to high school students. A review of examinees' performance on field-tested items represents a second check of the difficulty of reading selections on the various tests in the GED Test battery. A question may be rejected by either the test specialist or reviewers' estimates of the difficulty level of the examinees' demonstrated performance during the field test.

Cognitive Demands of Questions

The Language Arts, Reading, and Social Studies tests are solely classified according to an adaptation of Bloom's taxonomy (*Taxonomy of Educational Objectives Handbook 1: Cognitive Domain, 1956*). Questions on the *Science Test* are based on both a hierarchy outlined in the National Science Education Standards (NSES) and on Bloom's cognitive levels.

Questions on the Mathematics test are based on the National Assessment of Educational Progress (NAEP) levels of cognition.

A candidate's success on the GED Tests requires the use of higher-order thinking skills of analysis, synthesis, and evaluation. Following is a brief description of each cognitive level and corresponding skill:

Knowledge

Knowledge questions require the candidate to observe and recall information, including major ideas or concepts, and a basic mastery of subject matter. While the GED Tests do not assess basic recall of information, candidates should have knowledge of ideas and concepts that can be used in answering other questions.

Comprehension

Comprehension questions require the candidate to understand the meaning and intent of written and visual text. Comprehension questions measure the ability to:

- Understand and restate information
- Summarize ideas
- Translate knowledge into new contexts
- Make inferences
- Draw conclusions

Application

Application questions require the candidate to use information and ideas in a concrete situation. These questions measure the ability to:

- Use information in a new context
- Solve problems that require skills or knowledge

Other higher-order questions, such as those involving analysis or synthesis, require application as a part of the thinking process.

Analysis

Analysis questions require the candidate to break down information and to explore the relationship between ideas. These questions measure the ability to:

- Identify patterns
- Distinguish fact from opinion
- Recognize hidden or unstated meaning
- Identify cause and effect relationships
- Make a series of related inferences

All five content-cued tests require analytical skills, with a higher percentage of analysis questions found in the *Language Arts, Reading; Social Studies;* and *Science Tests.*

Synthesis

Synthesis questions require the candidate to produce information in the form of hypotheses, theories, stories, or compositions. Synthesis questions require the candidate to bring together pieces of information to create new ideas or thoughts. Synthesis questions measure the ability to:

- Use old ideas to create new ones
- Make generalizations based on given facts
- Relate knowledge from a variety of areas
- Make predictions based on information provided

One example of a synthesis question is the expository essay found in *Part II* of the *Language Arts, Writing Test.* In addition, synthesis questions are in both the *Language Arts, Reading* and *Science Tests.*

Evaluation

Evaluation questions require the candidate to make judgments about the validity and reliability of information based on criteria provided or assumed. These questions measure the ability to:

- Compare and discriminate among ideas
- Assess the value of theories, evidence, and presentations
- Make choices based on reasoned argument
- Recognize the role that values play in beliefs and decision making
- Indicate logical fallacies in arguments

Evaluation questions appear in both the *Social Studies* and *Science Tests.*

How to Use the Official GED Practice Tests

Guidelines for Using the Official GED Practice Tests

Guidelines outline the appropriate and inappropriate uses for the Official GED Practice Tests. It is important that individuals who use the test adhere to the guidelines for the appropriate uses.

Appropriate Uses of the Official GED Practice Tests

The Official GED Practice Tests **should** be used to:
- determine a candidate's readiness to take the actual GED Tests;
- provide practice in taking tests under standardized conditions similar to those encountered on the GED Tests; and
- reduce anxiety by increasing the candidate's familiarity with the types of questions found on the GED tests.

The Official GED Practice Tests are the ONLY true predictor of success on the GED Tests. While no one test or method of assessment should be used as the sole source of information for instruction, the Official GED Practice Tests can be useful in determining the effectiveness of a program of instruction. For example, if test results show that students are encountering problems with the essay portion of the *Language Arts, Writing Test,* program administrators and teachers may wish to identify strategies that could better assist students in improving their writing skills.

Inappropriate Uses of the Official GED Practice Tests

The Official GED Practice Tests **should not** be:
- administered to individuals who are known to be deficient in educational preparation and who may be discouraged from pursuing further education as a result of the testing experience;
- used as a graduation requirement at the end of an adult education program;
- given repeatedly to the same individual as a way of preparing for the actual GED Tests or for diagnostic purposes to identify areas of weakness; and
- used to evaluate the effectiveness of teachers; the evaluation of teachers is a complex process that requires more information than that provided through one standardized test.

Special Note to Teachers, Counselors, and Administrators

As with any standardized tests, there are limitations on the use of the Official GED Practice Tests and the results obtained. It is extremely important that teachers use their educational assessment skills and other outside evaluation procedures to plan a candidate's educational course of study.

Adult educators must be very sensitive to the needs of students taking the Official GED Practice Tests. Candidates should always be informed about the:
- purpose of the tests
- use of the tests
- limitations of the tests
- confidentiality of test scores

By keeping students informed, educators can ensure that students clearly understand the intent of the Official GED Practice Tests and how the test results can be used to assist them in evaluating their readiness to take the GED Tests.

The Practice Test Booklets

The Official GED Practice Tests format is similar to that of the actual GED Tests. There are six separate test booklets in an envelope. Directions are included for each subject area test. A sample question that illustrates the proper way to record answers is also included. The Official GED Practice Tests can be administered either individually or in a group setting.

The Official GED Practice Tests: Full-Length Test Form can be scored quickly by using the answer key provided with this booklet or the stencils provided with the package. Test results are reported on the same score scale as used by the actual full-length tests. This feature enables educators to easily compare a candidate's performance on the Practice Tests with the level of performance required in the state, territory, or province from which the GED credential will be issued.

In an effort to provide students with an experience that mirrors that of the full-length GED Tests, the Official GED Practice Test answer sheets are similar to those used in the official testing session. They provide students with an opportunity to see the type of answer sheet that will be used and to ask any questions about the correct recording of answers.

The answer sheet contains:
- numbered spaces for candidates to mark their answers to the multiple-choice questions;
- grids for candidates to record their responses to alternate format questions in *Mathematics Part I* and *Part II;* and
- two lined pages on which to write the essay for *Part II* of the *Language Arts, Writing Test.*

Administering the Tests

The Official GED Practice Tests must be administered in settings that mirror those of the actual GED Tests.

This guideline allows candidates an opportunity to gain experience in taking tests in standardized settings, as well as to determine how a candidate will perform in that type of setting.

To serve as a predictor, the Official GED Practice Tests must be administered using the recommended time limits for each subject area test. It is important to remember that candidates must adhere to strict time limits when taking the actual GED Tests. In fact, failure to adhere to the time limits of the Official Practice Tests is not fair to the candidate and may give him/her a distorted sense of how well he/she can perform on the GED Tests. The time limits allow candidates to work at a comfortable rate and still have time to complete the GED Tests.

The administrator of the Official GED Practice Tests (teacher, counselor, etc.) must be very careful when handling test materials. The Full-Length Test Form was developed specifically to simulate the GED testing situation as closely as possible. There are also seven half-length test forms of the Official GED Practice Tests, Forms PA–PG. It is important not to confuse the materials, answer keys, or conversion tables when working with the individual tests.

Scoring the Tests

After the candidate completes the Official GED Practice Tests: Full-Length Test Form, the multiple-choice and gridded response sections of the answer sheet may be scored using the answer keys or stencils. Before using the scoring stencil, the completed answer sheet should be scanned for any items where the candidate has marked more than one answer in order to avoid giving credit for any changed answers. Then the stencil should be placed over the answer sheet, aligning the hole for Full-Length Test Form with the filled-in bubble on the candidate's answer sheet. Correct answers showing through holes in the stencil will be counted as the raw score for each test. Alternate format question possible gridded responses for the *Mathematics Test* are provided on pages 17–18. The total number of correct answers for each test should be recorded in the RAW SCORE boxes on the answer sheet. Raw scores are then converted to GED standard scores to be recorded on the answer sheet.

Instructions for converting the number of correct answers to the GED standard score scale are provided in the conversion tables located on pages 12–15. It is very important that the appropriate conversion table is used. Conversion tables have been developed for each test of the Official GED Practice Tests. Using the wrong conversion table can result in erroneous scores.

The essay developed as *Part II* of the *Language Arts, Writing Test* should be scored using the guidelines provided on pages 63–66.

Scoring the Essay

Part II of the *Language Arts, Writing Test* requires the candidate to write an expository essay. Unlike the multiple-choice portion of the test, there is no answer key or stencil provided for scoring the essay.

Teachers may estimate the score that a student's writing should receive and use that estimate to calculate a composite score for the Language Arts, Writing Test. Information regarding the Essay Scoring Guide and instructions for using the scoring guide are provided on page 65. It is recommended that teachers thoroughly review the Essay Scoring Guide prior to estimating the score of a student's writing sample. With practice, teachers should be able to efficiently use the guide and feel comfortable in estimating a student's essay score.

A Word of Caution

Teachers scoring Official GED Practice Test essays have not had an opportunity to undergo the extensive and rigorous training as that required for readers for the actual GED Test. As a result, the total essay score should be regarded as only an estimate. Therefore, predictions based on the *Language Arts, Writing Test* standard score may be less precise than the score from the multiple-choice sections of the Official Practice Tests.

Analyzing and Interpreting Results of Official GED Practice Tests

The analysis and interpretation of results from the Official GED Practice Tests are important to candidates and instructors because they:

- provide information about the candidate's readiness for the actual full-length test; and
- indicate patterns of errors that may help determine a continuing course of GED preparation and study.

This section provides information to help educators interpret the candidate's results and suggest ways to use those results.

The GED Score Scale

The results of the Official GED Practice Tests are expressed on a scale ranging from 200 to 800. This same scale is used for the actual GED Tests. The answer key provides the correct responses for scoring the answer sheet. The GED standard scores correspond to the raw scores earned on an Official GED Practice Test. These scores are provided in conversion tables on pages 12–15. It is essential that the appropriate table be used based on the specific subject area test of the Official GED Practice Tests that has been taken.

The GED standard score scale is derived from the performance of approximately 10,000 graduating high school seniors. By comparing the GED standard scores obtained by the candidate on the Official GED Practice Test to the score requirements for passing the GED Tests, students and teachers can determine readiness to take the GED Tests. Minimum score requirements may vary from one jurisdiction to another. Check the score requirement for your area or jurisdiction.

Remember that any interpretations of results from the Official Practice Tests must be made using the GED standard scores—**not** raw scores. Raw scores are not comparable across subject areas. The reasons for this lack of comparability include:

- differences in the difficulty of questions across tests; and
- differences in the number of questions across tests.

Standard scores are comparable across subject area tests. Comparisons between subjects of the Official Practice Tests should only be made using Official GED standard scores.

Reliability

The reliability of a test refers to the consistency or stability of the test scores. A test that produces vastly different scores for the same individual on separate testing sessions, even when the individual has not changed substantially on the attribute being tested, does not produce reliable scores. A test is considered reliable when it produces similar scores for an individual on separate administrations.

To evaluate the reliability of test scores from the Official GED Practice Tests, the tests were administered to a nationally representative sample of graduating high school seniors in 2001. Using the obtained scores from these students, Kuder-Richardson internal consistency reliability coefficients (KR-20) were computed for each test form. These coefficients describe the extent to which all questions on a test correlate positively with one another. KR-20 coefficients range from 0 to 1. Larger coefficients reflect more reliable test scores.

Accuracy of Scores (The Standard Error of Measurement)

Even with a reliable test, there is always a slight deviation in predicting one test score based on another test score. As a result, there will usually be some difference between a candidate's Official Practice Test scores and his/her scores on the actual GED Tests. However, most candidates who take the Official GED Practice Tests want to know what score they are likely to earn on the GED Tests.

The standard error of measurement (SEM) is a numerical way of expressing how much a candidate's score can be expected to vary between the Official GED Practice Tests and the actual GED Tests. The SEM for two out of three examinees will be within (above or below) one SEM unit of his/her true score. For nearly all candidates, the test scores will be within two SEMs.

Although the SEM may vary according to subject area test, scores on the Official GED Practice Tests are generally within 50 standard score points on the GED Tests in any subject area. All candidates should be advised that their Official GED Practice Test scores are estimates and not an exact reflection of their final scores on the actual GED Tests.

Validity

All GED Tests and the Official GED Practice Tests are produced with the same content specifications, and all questions are matched as closely as possible on psychometric characteristics. This process ensures that the various test forms are very similar to one another. All new forms of the GED Tests are equated to the GED anchor form using the equipercentile method. This method is used to produce a relationship of equivalence between raw scores on two tests. This procedure ensures that the Official GED Practice Tests are valid for predicting future performance on the GED Tests.

Summary Profile of Student Performance

After all of the results have been converted to the GED score scale, they should be transferred to the Summary Profile section of the answer sheet. This profile provides an easy way to tally and compare Practice Test scores. Most jurisdictions require the development of an average GED score, and instructions are given for calculating this value.

Interpreting Test Results

Reporting Results to Individual Students

It is very important that test administrators take the time to review the results of the test with the student. GEDTS has provided complete Answer Explanations (Rationales) for each test question exclusively for the Full-Length Test Form. Administrators can use these thorough explanations on pages 19–61 to assist them in the review process.

- Review each test question the candidate missed. Determine if the candidate:
    - understood what was being asked;
    - experienced any problem with the test's vocabulary; or
    - experienced any problem with identifying a strategy for answering a question.
- Review each option offered for that question. Determine the reasons:
    - for the incorrect response; and
    - for eliminating incorrect choices.
- Review the test results according to the incorrect answers for each content cluster. Determine if the error patterns indicate a weakness that would require further instruction.
- Review the overall test performance on each subject. Determine if there are any patterns that may help in planning a course of study.

A careful review of the candidate's choices on incorrectly answered questions and on test performance by clusters should help the instructor determine whether or not a continued program of study is required. By using the steps listed above, the instructor can learn a lot about a candidate's:

- academic strengths and weaknesses;
- methods for interpreting questions;
- reasons for choosing specific responses; and
- study skills.

Evaluating Test Results for a Group of Students

Analysis of the test by the teacher and students as a group can also be a helpful process. Teachers may be able to identify reasons for particular difficulties within subject areas as well as with specific skills within those subject areas. The following is an explanation of how this process would work in the classroom.

First, identify a question by number and ask students who answered the question correctly to raise their hands. Next, record the number of students who answered each question on a copy of the test. Share with the group the numbers of the questions that many students missed. Next, ask which answers the students chose for the question, determine which answers were the most prevalent, and ask students why they chose those particular responses. It is especially helpful to students who chose different responses to present their reasons for doing so and try to convince one another of their correctness. Following the discussion, teachers may wish to ask how many students would choose each of the responses to each question.

Teachers who have used this technique have found that the best policy is to wait until the students have completed their discussion before explaining why a particular answer is correct. Students tend to stop paying attention and begin thinking about the next question if the teacher gives the correct answer immediately. This process works best when dealing with approximately ten questions in one class period.

Student debates over such questions are very revealing and rewarding. These discussions bring out the students' reasons for particular interpretations, which are often different from what the teacher expects. There is also evidence that students who participate in this type of process begin to read and analyze questions more carefully and thoroughly.

Questions and Answers About the Official GED Practice Tests

1. What is the grade level of the Official GED Practice Tests?

The GED Tests measure high school equivalency with passing score standards based on graduating high school seniors' performance. Students are tested in the spring of their senior year. The Official GED Practice Tests are developed and administered at the same time as the actual GED Tests. The GED standard score scale is derived from high school administrations and reflects the typical range of ability and cumulative knowledge existing in the graduating twelfth-grade population as a whole.

2. Are the Official GED Practice Tests primarily reading tests?

Reading competency alone will not enable the candidate to answer questions presented at the higher cognitive levels. The GED Tests require reading comprehension skills as a basis for all other skills assessed through the entire battery. As noted on page 6 of this manual, the GED Tests require students to *apply, analyze, synthesize,* and *evaluate* the information provided in the stimulus material and the test questions.

3. What is the reading level of the Official GED Practice Tests?

Questions used in the GED Tests are written or selected by practitioners: teachers and content experts current in that academic discipline. The questions are then screened through a process of review by at least three independent teachers and content experts and the GED test specialist who is a professional educator certified in that discipline. In this review, it is determined if the level of difficulty of the reading selection is appropriate for a high school graduate. Thus the "readability" of the questions on all of the GED Tests is monitored early in the test development process through the judgment of experienced educators.

After questions have survived the first stage of screening, they are field-tested through administration to high school students. A review of examinees' performance on field-tested items represents a second check of the difficulty of the reading selection on the various tests in the GED Test battery. A question may be rejected by either the test specialist or reviewers' estimates of the difficulty level, or by the examinees' demonstrated performance during the field test.

4. How should candidates prepare for the GED Tests?

Candidates can prepare for the GED Tests in a variety of ways. There is a wide range of programs available, usually at little or no cost, throughout the U.S. and Canada. Teachers working with GED instructors can obtain information from the GED Testing Service about the GED Tests and the knowledge and skills required for the tests. In addition, local, state, and provincial programs produce teachers' manuals of their own which offer specific suggestions for helping students prepare for the GED Tests. The GED Testing Service website **www.gedtest.org** also provides information for candidates and GED program providers.

5. Why should candidates follow the time limits?

The actual GED Tests are administered using time limits. By using the prescribed time limits for the Official GED Practice Tests, candidates have an opportunity to see how well they will perform under conditions similar to those they will encounter on the actual full-length GED Tests.

6. How high must a candidate score to succeed on the Official GED Practice Tests?

The GED Testing Service sets minimum passing scores for the full-length GED tests. Each state, territory, or province defines its own criteria that can equal or exceed the GEDTS minimum score, and it establishes a clear policy on standards for passing the GED Tests. Generally, a candidate would be expected to exceed the standard established for the actual GED Tests by the state, territory, or province. If a candidate's scores on the Practice Tests barely meet state minimum requirements, the Standard Error of Measurement should be taken into consideration and additional instruction is recommended.

7. How close are the estimated GED Scores on the Practice Tests to the scores that may be obtained on the actual GED Tests?

Information is provided on page 9 about the standard score points that can be expected for most candidates. In most cases, the difference between the standard scores on the actual GED Tests and the Practice Tests is less than 10 GED standard score points. The margin may be slightly larger for the *Language Arts, Writing Test* depending on how accurately the essay is scored.

U.S. English Full-Length Test Form Conversion Table: Language Arts, Writing

To determine the *Language Arts, Writing* standard score:
1. Locate the number of questions the candidate answered correctly on *Part I*, the multiple-choice section of the test, in the column at the far left.
2. From that point, move horizontally across the table until you intersect the column with the candidate's estimated essay score (*Part II*). If two readers have scored the essay, an average of the two scores should be calculated.
3. The number at the intersection of the row with the appropriate multiple-choice score and the column with the appropriate estimated essay score is the *Language Arts, Writing* standard score.

U.S. English Full-Length Test Form: Language Arts, Writing

Number of Correct Answers on Part I (Multiple Choice)	2	2.5	Part II Score (Essay Score) 3	3.5	4
50	670	710	760	800	800
49	630	680	720	770	800
48	590	640	690	730	800
47	560	600	650	700	770
46	530	570	620	670	740
45	500	550	600	640	710
44	480	530	580	620	690
43	470	520	560	610	680
42	460	500	550	600	670
41	450	490	540	590	660
40	440	490	530	580	650
39	430	480	520	570	640
38	420	470	520	560	630
37	420	460	510	560	630
36	410	460	500	550	620
35	400	450	500	540	610
34	400	450	490	540	610
33	390	440	490	530	600
32	390	440	480	530	600
31	380	430	480	520	590
30	380	430	470	520	590
29	380	420	470	520	590
28	370	420	470	510	580
27	370	420	460	510	580
26	370	410	460	510	580

© 2008, American Council on Education/The GED Testing Service

U.S. English Full-Length Test Form Conversion Table: Language Arts, Writing (continued)

U.S. English Full-Length Test Form: Language Arts, Writing

Number of Correct Answers on Part I (Multiple Choice)	\multicolumn{5}{c}{Part II Score (Essay Score)}
	2	2.5	3	3.5	4
25	360	410	460	500	570
24	360	410	450	500	570
23	360	400	450	500	570
22	350	400	450	490	560
21	350	400	440	490	560
20	350	390	440	490	560
19	340	390	440	480	550
18	340	390	430	480	550
17	340	380	430	480	550
16	330	380	420	470	540
15	330	370	420	470	540
14	320	370	410	460	530
13	310	360	410	450	520
12	310	350	400	450	520
11	300	340	390	440	510
10	290	330	380	430	500
9	270	320	370	410	480
8	260	310	350	400	470
7	240	290	330	380	450
6	220	270	320	360	430
5	220	270	320	360	430
4	220	270	320	360	430
3	220	270	320	360	430
2	220	270	320	360	430
1	220	270	320	360	430

© 2008, American Council on Education/The GED Testing Service

U.S. English Full-Length Test Form Conversion Tables: Language Arts, Reading and Social Studies

To determine the standard score for *Language Arts, Reading; Social Studies; Science;* and *Mathematics*:

1. Locate the number of questions the candidate answered correctly on the multiple-choice section of the test, in the column at the far left.
2. Read the corresponding standard score from the column on the right.

Compare the candidate's standard scores to the minimum score requirements in the jurisdiction in which the GED credential is to be issued.

U.S. English Full-Length Test Form: Language Arts, Reading

Number of Correct Answers	Estimated GED Test Standard Score
40	800
39	790
38	740
37	680
36	630
35	590
34	560
33	530
32	510
31	490
30	480
29	470
28	460
27	460
26	450
25	440
24	440
23	430
22	430
21	420
20	420
19	410
18	400
17	400
16	390
15	390
14	380
13	370
12	360
11	350
10	340
9	330
8	310
7	300
6	280
5	260
4	240
3	210
2	200
1	200

U.S. English Full-Length Test Form: Social Studies

Number of Correct Answers	Estimated GED Test Standard Score
50	800
49	800
48	770
47	700
46	640
45	590
44	560
43	550
42	540
41	530
40	520
39	510
38	510
37	500
36	490
35	480
34	480
33	470
32	460
31	450
30	440
29	430
28	420
27	410
26	400
25	390
24	380
23	380
22	370
21	370
20	360
19	350
18	350
17	340
16	330
15	320
14	310
13	300
12	290
11	280
10	270
9	260
8	250
7	230
6	220
5	210
4	200
3	200
2	200
1	200

© 2008, American Council on Education/The GED Testing Service

U.S. English Full-Length Test Form Conversion Tables: Science and Mathematics, Parts I and II

U.S. English Full-Length Test Form: Science	
Number of Correct Answers	Estimated GED Test Standard Score
50	800
49	730
48	680
47	650
46	610
45	590
44	570
43	550
42	540
41	530
40	520
39	500
38	490
37	480
36	470
35	470
34	460
33	450
32	440
31	440
30	430
29	420
28	420
27	410
26	410
25	400
24	390
23	390
22	380
21	370
20	370
19	360
18	350
17	340
16	330
15	330
14	320
13	310
12	300
11	300
10	290
9	280
8	270
7	260
6	250
5	240
4	230
3	210
2	200
1	200

U.S. English Full-Length Test Form: Mathematics	
Number of Correct Answers	Estimated GED Test Standard Score
50	800
49	720
48	680
47	650
46	610
45	590
44	560
43	540
42	530
41	520
40	510
39	490
38	480
37	470
36	460
35	440
34	430
33	420
32	410
31	400
30	390
29	380
28	370
27	360
26	350
25	340
24	330
23	330
22	320
21	310
20	300
19	300
18	290
17	280
16	270
15	270
14	260
13	250
12	250
11	240
10	230
9	230
8	220
7	210
6	210
5	200
4	200
3	200
2	200
1	200

© 2008, American Council on Education/The GED Testing Service

U.S. English Full-Length Test Form: Answer Key

Language Arts, Writing		Language Arts, Reading		Social Studies		Science	
1. 2	26. 3	1. 3	21. 5	1. 2	26. 4	1. 4	26. 2
2. 5	27. 2	2. 4	22. 3	2. 3	27. 1	2. 2	27. 1
3. 2	28. 1	3. 3	23. 5	3. 5	28. 2	3. 5	28. 3
4. 3	29. 4	4. 5	24. 4	4. 4	29. 4	4. 3	29. 3
5. 3	30. 5	5. 4	25. 3	5. 3	30. 3	5. 2	30. 4
6. 4	31. 4	6. 2	26. 5	6. 2	31. 5	6. 2	31. 3
7. 1	32. 2	7. 5	27. 4	7. 3	32. 2	7. 5	32. 5
8. 1	33. 2	8. 4	28. 1	8. 1	33. 3	8. 5	33. 5
9. 2	34. 5	9. 4	29. 4	9. 4	34. 3	9. 4	34. 2
10. 3	35. 3	10. 4	30. 2	10. 1	35. 5	10. 3	35. 3
11. 3	36. 4	11. 1	31. 2	11. 3	36. 1	11. 4	36. 4
12. 1	37. 5	12. 5	32. 1	12. 2	37. 3	12. 5	37. 3
13. 2	38. 5	13. 2	33. 3	13. 4	38. 1	13. 2	38. 1
14. 4	39. 2	14. 3	34. 1	14. 1	39. 5	14. 4	39. 2
15. 2	40. 3	15. 3	35. 5	15. 5	40. 2	15. 2	40. 1
16. 3	41. 5	16. 4	36. 1	16. 4	41. 4	16. 3	41. 1
17. 5	42. 2	17. 3	37. 3	17. 2	42. 5	17. 3	42. 4
18. 5	43. 3	18. 2	38. 1	18. 1	43. 3	18. 1	43. 2
19. 3	44. 1	19. 1	39. 2	19. 2	44. 4	19. 1	44. 3
20. 5	45. 1	20. 1	40. 2	20. 5	45. 1	20. 4	45. 2
21. 2	46. 5			21. 3	46. 4	21. 1	46. 3
22. 1	47. 1			22. 5	47. 5	22. 3	47. 5
23. 4	48. 3			23. 2	48. 1	23. 1	48. 3
24. 4	49. 2			24. 4	49. 2	24. 1	49. 4
25. 4	50. 4			25. 1	50. 2	25. 5	50. 2

U.S. English Full-Length Test Form: Answer Key

Mathematics

Note: For questions 3, 4, 10, 16, 17, 23, 31, and 43, several examples of how the answer could be gridded are shown.

Part I
1. 3
2. 4
3.

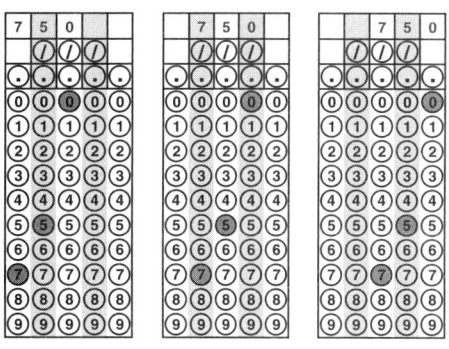

4.

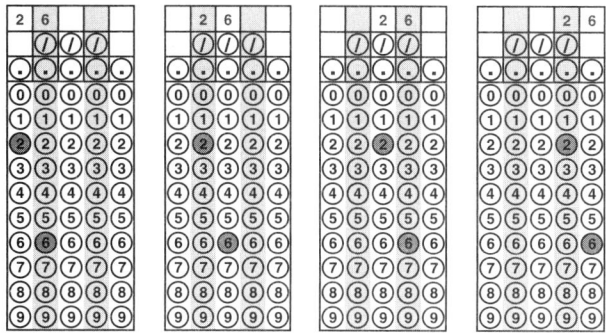

5. 3
6. 1
7. 5
8. 4
9. 5
10.

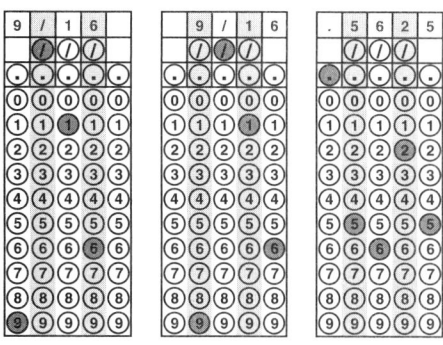

11. 2
12. 1
13. 2
14. 2
15. 4
16.

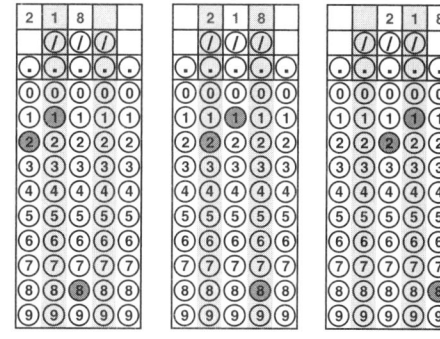

17.

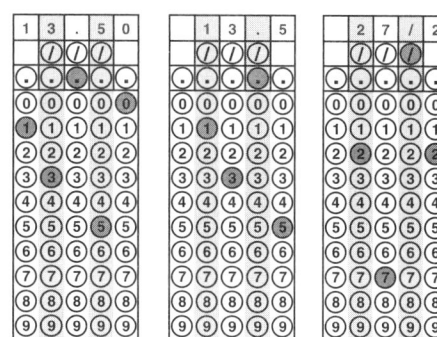

18. 3
19. 2
20. 4
21. 4
22. 5
23.

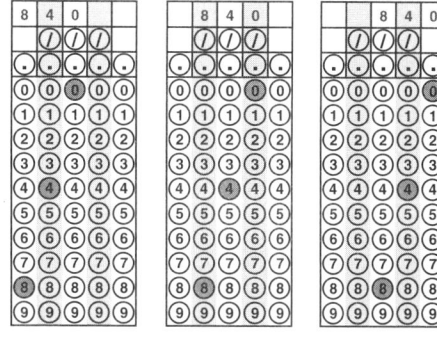

24. 5   25. 3   26. 1

U.S. English Full-Length Test Form: Answer Key (continued)

Mathematics

Part II
27. 4
28. 3
29. 5
30. 2
31.

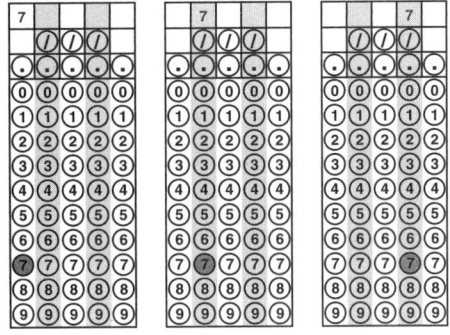

32. 5
33. 3
34. 4
35.

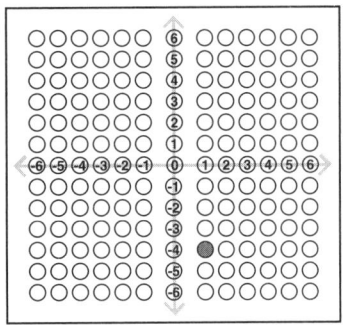

36. 3
37. 1
38. 2

Note: For question 35, the answer is the ordered pair (1, -4) as shown on the coordinate grid.

39. 1
40. 3
41. 2
42. 5

43.

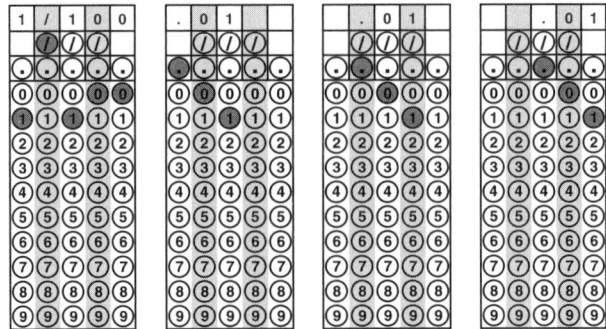

44. 3
45. 4
46. 1
47.

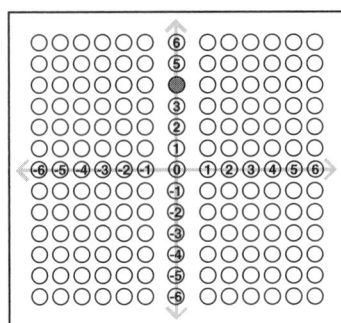

48. 5
49. 2
50. 4

Note: For question 47, the answer is the ordered pair (0, 4) as shown on the coordinate grid.

18 Official GED Practice Tests Administrator's Guide: Full-Length Test Form

ANSWER EXPLANATIONS (RATIONALES) FOR EACH TEST QUESTION

Language Arts, Writing

*Exclusively provided and written by the GED Testing Service, answer explanations (rationales) for each test question are provided here for the Full-Length Official GED Practice Test.

1.
   (1) This answer is plausible because the opening dependent/subordinate clause contains a subject (you) and verb (know); consequently, a test taker may see the dependent and independent clauses as two complete sentences.
   (2) This answer is correct because the dependent/subordinate clause begins the sentence; therefore, it must be followed by a comma.
   (3) This answer is plausible because a test taker may see two separate ideas being joined by "and": "you know" and "One was involved."
   (4) This answer is plausible because a test taker sees two separate ideas or independent clauses; however, the person confuses the present participle verb form "knowing" with the present tense form "know."
   (5) This answer is plausible because the verb in the independent clause is in the past tense (was), and a test taker may assume that the verb in the opening clause should also be past tense (have known).

2.
   (1) This answer is plausible because a test taker may be more familiar with the spelling "least;" however, this is the incorrect homophone form.
   (2) This answer is plausible because the test taker may see "expense" as the subject of the verb "are intended;" thus the comma would not be needed.
   (3) This answer is plausible because a test taker may confuse the incorrect homophone form "lodes" for the correct form "loads."
   (4) This answer is plausible because a test taker may see the subject and verb "we were hired" needing a comma to separate the introductory words before them.
   (5) This answer is correct because the commas set off the nonessential phrase "leased at considerable expense."

3.
   (1) This answer is plausible because a test taker may feel that the action of the accident was in the past, so all other actions in the memorandum must also be in the past.
   (2) This answer is correct because the memorandum conveys procedures to follow in the continuing present, so the present form of the verb is required as is its plural number to agree with "they."
   (3) This answer is plausible because the subject is plural, and a test taker may assume incorrectly that "s" is needed to make the verb plural.
   (4) This answer is plausible because the verb tense "to have been kept" conveys the continuity of an action from past to present. A test taker may see the verb use as correct.
   (5) This answer is plausible because the progressive verb tense "to be keeping" conveys the continuity of an action in the present time. A test taker may see the verb use as correct.

4.
   (1) This answer is plausible because the test taker may see "engine maintenance" as part of the "Oil and filter changes."
   (2) This answer is plausible because a test taker may see "Oil and filter changes" in the engine, and "maintenance" would be a separate item in the list.
   (3) This answer is correct because the sentence contains a list of three items that are the company's responsibility. Commas are needed to separate each of the three items.
   (4) This answer is plausible because the test taker may see "changes engine maintenance" as a separate item.
   (5) This answer is plausible because a test taker may see "Oil" and "filter," as separate items.

5.
   (1) This answer is plausible because a test taker may not see the policy taking effect in the future but in the present "maintain."
   (2) This answer is plausible because a test taker may see "maintaining a mileage chart" as describing the "employee." However, using "maintaining" without a helping verb leaves the sentence without a verb.
   (3) This answer is correct because the memorandum discusses a policy that will be implemented in the near future.
   (4) This answer is plausible because a test taker may not see "records" as a verb form but incorrectly as a noun.
   (5) This answer is plausible because a test taker may see the clause "which maintains a mileage chart recording" as referring to the "employee." However, by inserting "which," the subject "employee" no longer has a verb.

6.
   (1) This answer is plausible because a test taker may see the example as two sentences.
   (2) This answer is plausible because a test taker may see the example as two sentences. However, the second sentence begins with "To."
   (3) This answer is plausible because test takers may view "receipts" as part of a list that includes "mileage claims" and the concluding clause.
   (4) This answer is correct because "which they must submit also" is redundant. Since the sentence reads, "employees will be expected to submit fuel receipts and mileage claims," there is no other item to be submitted, so the "also" is not needed.
   (5) This answer is plausible because test takers may see the sentence clearly making sense as written. However, the final clause is confusing.

7.
   (1) This answer is correct because the verb "will have been" refers to two future actions (i.e. some future action would occur after another future action "will have been"). There is only the single action "will be."

(2) This answer is plausible because a test taker may not be aware that parenthetical words, words that interrupt the sentence's flow, need commas before and after them. "However" is a common parenthetical.
(3) This answer is plausible because a test taker may assume that the program to maintain "a good driving record" is ongoing. "Maintaining" is the progressive or ongoing form of the verb.
(4) This answer is plausible because a test taker may see "for" used as a conjunction to convey that what follows is the reason that an employee "maintain a good driving record."
(5) This answer is plausible because a test taker may see the need to provide a direct object for "keep."

8.
(1) This answer is correct because the rewritten sentence uses active voice ("employee will cover") of the verb, improving the original sentence which uses passive voice ("increase will be covered").
(2) This answer is plausible because a test taker may read this choice as an increase resulting from "accidents" and not an increase in accidents as written.
(3) This answer is plausible because a test taker may see the increase as accidental on the employee's part.
(4) This answer is plausible because a test taker may read the sentence as listing three incidents caused by the employee's driving.
(5) This answer is plausible because the verbs are expressed in parallel form. A test taker may see two effects of accidents and driving infraction (i.e. the employee will cover and will result).

9.
(1) This answer is plausible because a test taker may see the eight proper nouns and assume that the item is testing capitalization.
(2) This answer is correct because a comma does not follow the verb in a sentence, separating the objects or complements.
(3) This answer is plausible because a test taker may see that the three inventors are grouped together rather than listed separately,
(4) This answer is plausible because a test taker may assume that the comma after "are" and the comma after "Franklin" are to set "Benjamin Franklin" off from the rest of the sentence.
(5) This answer is plausible because a test taker may see the eight proper nouns and assume that the item is testing capitalization.

10.
(1) This answer is plausible because it is a complete sentence; however, it does not cover the supporting sentences in paragraph B.
(2) This answer is plausible because the sentence structure is correct, but the sentence's content doesn't cover the supporting sentences in paragraph B.
(3) This answer is correct because it provides a topic sentence for paragraph B.
(4) This answer is plausible because a test taker may see it as the topic sentence. However, the sentence is written in passive voice. "Benjamin Franklin," not "man" is the subject of the verb "was."

(5) This answer is plausible because a test taker may think that all of the details relate to the accomplishments of Benjamin Franklin, but paragraph B lacks a topic sentence.

11.
(1) This answer is plausible because a test taker may see "Alexander Graham Bell" as the subject and "born" as the verb; therefore, a comma would not be used to separate the two.
(2) This answer is plausible because a test taker may see "born in 1847," ignoring "in scotland," as an appositive.
(3) This answer is correct because the "s" in the proper noun "Scotland" needs to be capitalized.
(4) This answer is plausible because a test taker may see "united states" as a descriptive, generic term, not the 50 states united as a country.
(5) This answer is plausible because a test taker may feel that the phrase "in 1871" has a close relationship with the rest of the sentence and needs a comma.

12.
(1) This is the correct answer because the singular pronoun "he" requires the singular verb "was."
(2) This answer is plausible because a test taker assumes that there is a comparison of the inventors.
(3) This answer is plausible because the test taker may feel that the verb needs to be followed by an adverb "mostly." However, "most" correctly conveys the superlative degree of "famous."
(4) This answer is plausible because a test taker may feel that the phrase "of the telephone" has a close relationship with the rest of the sentence and needs a comma.
(5) This answer is plausible because the sentence is structurally a sentence (i.e., subject, verb, complement). A test taker may see it correct as written.

13.
(1) This answer is plausible because a test taker may notice the progressive verb (ending in -ing) "while working" at the beginning of the sentence and feel that all verbs must be consistent.
(2) This is the correct answer because the actions took place in the past; therefore, the past tense form of the verb is needed.
(3) This answer is plausible because a test taker may feel that the emphatic form of the verb is needed to emphasize Bell's experiments.
(4) This answer is plausible because a test taker may assume incorrectly that the habitual action conveyed by the verb "would have been performing" meant that Bell had been successful in his experiments before working on transmitting speech. However, the actions occurred simultaneously in the past.
(5) This answer is plausible because a test taker may feel that "would be performing" suggests that Bell had not been "performing basic experiments" before his "working" on transmitting speech.

14.
(1) This answer is plausible because a test taker may assume that months of the year, like seasons of the year, are not capitalized.
(2) This answer is plausible because a test taker may see the adverb clause that follows "1876" as restrictive (i.e., limiting the success). However, it is a nonrestrictive clause adding more information about the "Success."

- (3) This answer is plausible because a test taker may see the comma as needed to prevent misreading and to emphasize the quote.
- **(4) This is the correct answer because the sentence refers to a time in the past, March 10, 1876. Therefore, the past form of the verb "was" is required.**
- (5) This answer is plausible because the quote refers to a time in the past, and a test taker may assume "came" is the correct verb form for the quote.

15.
- (1) This answer is plausible because a test taker may see the progression of different inventions, failing to notice that the second group (beginning with "after") is a complete sentence.
- **(2) This answer is correct because "after" begins a second independent clause or complete sentence. Writing sentence 15 as two complete sentences conveys two separate sets of inventions.**
- (3) This answer is plausible because it establishes sentence 15 as two complete sentences; however, the "and" is not needed.
- (4) This answer is plausible because a test taker may see that all that the words need is a transition ("then") to convey the stages of invention.
- (5) This answer is plausible because a test taker may believe that "thereafter" may sound like an effective transition.

16.
- (1) This answer is plausible because a test taker may see each item in the list of five as a separate "discovery," not looking at all five.
- (2) This answer is plausible because a test taker may not distinguish among the items listed in this sentence.
- **(3) This is the correct answer because the sentence lists Bell's inventions. Because "phonograph" is the second item in a list of five items, it must be followed by a comma.**
- (4) This answer is plausible because "and" may be used in place of a comma to emphasize each item in a list, so a test taker may see the insertion of "and" emphasizing the last two items in the list.
- (5) This answer is plausible because a test taker may overlook the missing comma or misread the five separate items.

17.
- (1) This answer is plausible because a test taker may believe that a comma is acceptable in separating two independent clauses/sentences.
- (2) This answer is plausible because a test taker may see a contrast (indicated by "but") between the two independent clauses/sentences.
- (3) This answer is plausible because a test taker may see the addition of "truthfully" as an improvement to the sentence. However, it is a superficial change that has not corrected the comma splice.
- (4) This answer is plausible because a test taker sees correctly that two independent clauses/sentences are separated by a comma. However, in accepted usage, the conjunction "and" when preceded by a comma, joins two sentences into one. It is not used as a conjunctive adverb (like "however") to serve as a transition beginning a sentence.
- **(5) This answer is correct because a period is needed to separate two independent clauses/sentences.**

18.
- (1) This answer is plausible because a test taker may see the sentence identifying three items needed by the writer of the letter.
- (2) This answer is plausible because a test taker may confuse the birth certificate with the Social Security card/ID.
- (3) This answer is plausible because a test taker may see two reasons for the writer's request: "to apply and to need." This answer is incorrect because the sentence will not have a verb.
- (4) This answer is plausible because a test taker may see the expression "but the reason why is because" as appropriate because it explains why the writer needs the birth certificate." However, the conjunction "but" indicates that what follows is an alternative.
- **(5) This answer is correct because the beginning independent clause is followed by three phrases after the period. The phrases refer to the reason why a "copy of the birth certificate is needed."**

19.
- (1) This answer is plausible because a test taker may assume that because both verbs ("advised" and "contacted") are in the past tense, an improved sentence is the result.
- (2) This answer is plausible because a test taker may see another person ("you") whom "They advised."
- **(3) This answer is correct because the first person pronoun "me" refers to the author of the letter, and he was the person advised "to contact" the Office of Vital Records.**
- (4) This answer is plausible because a test taker may misread the sentence that "by contacting" the writer will obtain his birth certificate.
- (5) This answer is plausible because a test taker may see "them" as a generic contact. However, the "you" "They advised to contact" is the Office of Vital Records.

20.
- (1) This answer is plausible because a test taker may not see the comma after "First" as necessary; however, its use is consistent with the other transition ("Second") to indicate the author's explanations.
- (2) This answer is plausible because a test taker may see the words "all though" as the correct spelling.
- (3) This answer is plausible because a test taker may see "Michael" as being so closely connected with his full name that a comma is unnecessary.
- (4) This answer is plausible because a test taker may see the need to separate the subject from the verb.
- **(5) This answer is correct because the commas are appropriate after the introductory word "First" and after "Michael" in the introductory adverb clause.**

21.
- (1) This answer is plausible because a test taker may assume that the subject "I" is understood. However, the "understood" subject is used with the second person, not the first.
- **(2) This answer is correct because as written "Having used Michael most of my life" is a fragment. Adding the subject pronoun "I" and changing the verb to the present form, rather than the present participle, creates an independent clause/sentence.**

(3) This answer is plausible because a test taker may not see the comma and "so" as a conjunction joining two independent clauses/sentences but as a modifier in the introductory fragment.
(4) This answer is plausible because a test taker may see "with the exception of my birth certificate" as an addition to "all my records."
(5) This answer is plausible because a test taker may see the plural "records" needing a plural pronoun as subject of the plural verb "are."

22.
(1) This answer is correct because the sentence provides a topic sentence to organize the details in paragraph B.
(2) This answer is plausible because a test taker may understand the writer's attempt to clarify how "Michael" is really his middle name, not his first.
(3) This answer is plausible because a test taker may see that the first independent clause/sentence in this compound sentence would be a valid topic sentence. However, the second sentence in the compound sentence is irrelevant.
(4) This answer is plausible because a test taker may assume that the writer does not use his given first name because of a conflict with his parents, who gave him that name.
(5) This answer is plausible because a test taker may assume that the writer needs to explain why he uses his middle name. However, his intent is to provide the information to help locate his records.

23.
(1) This answer is plausible because a test taker may feel that "accordingly" sounds like a better word to follow the transition "Second."
(2) This answer is plausible because a test taker may not see the need for using the comma to separate the introductory phrase from the subject and verb "types…is."
(3) This answer is plausible because a test taker assumes that the writer is requesting only one type of document, a birth certificate, so the singular "type" is needed.
(4) This answer is correct because the subject of the sentence is "types," which is plural. Therefore, the plural verb form "are" is required.
(5) This answer is plausible because a test taker may see "acceptable" as a form of the verb "accept." Therefore, the verb "is" would not be needed.

24.
(1) This answer is plausible because a test taker may see this sentence directed to the official in the Office of Vital Records. Therefore, "you" would be seen as appropriate.
(2) This answer is plausible because a test taker may see the conditional action (thinking that the certified copy was most useful) was in the past.
(3) This answer is plausible because a test taker may feel that since "copies" is used in the first instance, it needs to be used in the second instance as well.
(4) This answer is correct because the writer assumes and doesn't know positively that the "certified copy" is most useful, so the verb's action needs to be conditional, using "would."
(5) This answer is plausible because a test taker may think that what the Office of Vital Records is currently using applies to the present, not the past.

25.
(1) This answer is plausible because a test taker may see the letter beginning with paragraph B. Paragraph B begins with the transition "First," which may draw test takers to that choice.
(2) This answer is plausible because a test taker may see the information in paragraph E as not needed in the letter. Since paragraph E does not deal with the need for the document or the possible confusion with the writer's name, it may be seen as unnecessary.
(3) This answer is plausible because a test taker may see both paragraphs related to the request for a birth certificate in order to apply for Social Security.
(4) This answer is correct because both paragraphs C and D discuss the requirements for the birth certificate that will be accepted by the Social Security office.
(5) This answer is plausible because a test taker may see both paragraphs specifying the type of certificate needed and payment for it. Therefore, both paragraphs should be joined.

26.
(1) This answer is plausible because a test taker may feel that a comma is needed to separate the clause ("that the company will fill …") from "you," indirect object of the infinitive.
(2) This answer is plausible because a test taker may confuse the correct homonym for "four."
(3) This answer is correct because a comma is not used to separate a noun clause ("that the company will fill …") when used as the direct object of the infinitive "to inform."
(4) This answer is plausible because a test taker may confuse the commonly misspelled "feel" for "fill."
(5) This answer is plausible because a test taker may assume that "that the company" refers to "you," which may be seen as the subject of the verb "will fill."

27.
(1) This answer is plausible because a test taker may assume that a clause ("that employees is needed") identifies what is meant by additional.
(2) This answer is correct because the subject "employees" requires the plural verb "are."
(3) This answer is plausible because a test taker may assume that the process of filling new positions is an ongoing process requiring the progressive verb form "is needing."
(4) This answer is plausible because a test taker may read the sentence with "meeting our increased volume of business" as a gerund phrase completing "is needed." The gerund phrase provides a result that the additional employees will provide.
(5) This answer is plausible because a test taker may view the volume of business increasing over time; therefore, the adverb "increasingly" refers to the infinitive "to meet."

28.
(1) This answer is correct because the revision changes the passive voice verb "will be assigned" to active voice "Supervisors will assign."
(2) This answer is plausible because a test taker may see "employees" as the direct object of the verb "will assign."
(3) This answer is plausible because a test taker may see "respective duty offices" as the direct object of the verb "will assign."

- (4) This answer is plausible because a test taker may see "offices, duties, respect" as the direct objects of the verb "will assign."
- (5) This answer is plausible because a test taker may see "specific" and "duties" describing what the "Supervisors will assign."

29.
- (1) This answer is plausible because a test taker may see the prepositional phrase "About company benefits" as an independent clause/complete sentence.
- (2) This answer is plausible because a test taker may see the prepositional phrase "About company benefits" as a fragment but feel making it a relative clause will correct the error. However, the relative clause would incorrectly describe "employees."
- (3) This answer is plausible because a test taker may incorrectly see the need for revising the prepositional phrase "About company benefits" as a clause, but as a nonrestrictive clause requiring a comma before it.
- **(4) This answer is correct because sentence 8 is a prepositional phrase and a fragment. Because the phrase describes the verb "will inform," it follows at the end of the sentence without a comma.**
- (5) This answer is plausible because a test taker may see "About company benefits" and "prospective employees" as two additional pieces of information.

30.
- (1) This answer is plausible because a test taker may understand that the interviews are currently in progress; therefore, the progressive verb form "taking place." However, the helping verb "are" is needed to define the tense.
- (2) This answer is plausible because a test taker may assume that the interviews "had taken place" earlier.
- (3) This answer is plausible because a test taker may think that the present infinitive "to take" indicates a future time. However, "to take" expresses an action following another action—there is no other previous action.
- (4) This answer is plausible because a test taker may feel that the interviews began in the past and will still be held.
- **(5) This answer is correct because the interviews "will take place" later in the future, so the verb must be in the future tense.**

31.
- (1) This answer is plausible because a test taker may see the need to directly address the director who must "review and return" the recommendations. In this imperative sentence, the "you" is understood but not written. Also, if "You" were being used in direct address, it should be followed by a comma.
- (2) This answer is plausible because a test taker may feel that the verb "review" needs to be in parallel form with "returning."
- (3) This answer is plausible because a test taker may see two independent clauses/sentences needed to express what the writer expects of the director (review and return).
- **(4) This answer is correct because the writer of the letter is asking the company director to "review" her recommendation and "return" them to her. The two actions required of the director must be in parallel construction.**
- (5) This answer is plausible because a test taker may see the pronoun "you" emphasizing the director who needs to return the recommendations. However, the possessive form of the pronoun is required before a gerund.

32.
- (1) This answer is plausible because a test taker may see all of the key words from the original sentence; however, they are arranged differently. Also, a comma is used to set off introductory words from the independent clause/sentence.
- **(2) This answer is correct because the sentence is written in the active voice "Your prompt attention is." Also, the phrase "to this matter" is correctly placed after the word it modifies, "attention." The reader can easily follow the writer's thought in this sentence.**
- (3) This answer is plausible because a test taker may feel that placing the emphatic idea "your prompt attention" at the end of the sentence is an effective revision.
- (4) This answer is plausible because a test taker may assume that the qualifiers "prompt and greatly appreciated" refer to "attention." Therefore, this revision would improve the sentence. However, it is the "prompt attention" that the writer will "greatly appreciate(d)."
- (5) This answer is plausible because a test taker may see all of the key words from the original sentence; however, they are arranged differently. Also, a comma is used to set off introductory words from the independent clause/sentence.

33.
- (1) This answer is plausible because a test taker may think that the director is a singular person; therefore, a singular verb "has" would create subject-verb agreement.
- **(2) This answer is correct because "further" is used to indicate an additional quantity of information, whereas "farther" would be used for an additional distance.**
- (3) This answer is plausible because a test taker may see "information" as the last word in the introductory adverb clause. The last word in an introductory adverb clause is followed by a comma.
- (4) This answer is plausible because a test taker may assume that "upon" suggests when the reader of the letter "comes upon" a questions, he or she will contact the writer.
- (5) This answer is plausible because a test taker may feel that the comma needs to be placed earlier in the sentence to set off the long string of compound verbs, introductory clause, and prepositional phrase.

34.
- (1) This answer is plausible because a test taker may feel that the content of paragraphs A and B both refer to the additional employees. However, paragraph A refers to the need, and paragraph B refers to the process.
- (2) This answer is plausible because a test taker may feel that the interview process, described in paragraph C, develops the types of employees needed as described in paragraph B. However, paragraph B refers to the specific position needs and the role of the supervisors with the new employees. The interview process is not related to paragraph B's focus.
- (3) This answer is plausible because a test taker may see all of the essential details in paragraphs B and C. However, sentence 3 of paragraph A sets the focus for the memorandum.

(4) This answer is plausible because a test taker may see all of the essential details in paragraphs A and C. However, sentence 4 of paragraph B states the specific positions that will be hired, following up with the focus statement in paragraph A.
(5) **This answer is correct because sentence 9 is the topic sentence for paragraph C, which lists details of the interview process.**

35.
(1) This answer is plausible because a test taker may assume that since the article is based on earlier research, the past tense "was" is needed.
(2) This answer is plausible because a test taker may think that the search "to find individuals" is ongoing. Therefore, the progressive form of the verb "finding" is needed.
(3) **This is the correct answer because the subordinate/dependent/relative clause requires a verb that agrees with "individuals." "Feeling" cannot be the verb because it does not have helping verbs that would make a participle a subject's verb.**
(4) This answer is plausible because a test taker who thinks that "feeling" is the correct form would conclude that "exhausting" would be parallel in form.
(5) This answer is plausible because a test taker may not see the incorrect verb form as an error.

36.
(1) This answer is plausible because a test taker may feel that a "who" clause is needed to specify the adults needing a nap because they lack energy.
(2) This answer is plausible because a test taker may feel that a participle phrase "feeling a sudden lack of energy" is needed to specify which adults need a nap.
(3) This answer is plausible because a test taker may think that the participle "lacking" is needed to describe "adults." However, the noun "lack" is needed to complete the subject and the verb.
(4) **This answer is correct because a comma is not needed for the prepositional phrase "after a large lunch" that follows the subject, verb, and complements.**
(5) This answer is plausible because a test taker might recognize that the clause "that follows a large lunch" would be correct. However, the comma would still need to be removed (as in #4) because clauses beginning with "that" do not have commas before them.

37.
(1) This answer is plausible because a test taker might think that "believing" is needed as a participle describing "researchers." However, "believe" is the verb for the subject "researchers."
(2) This answer is plausible because a test taker may see "to improve" as a prepositional phrase and not an infinitive. If "to" were a preposition, it would require the noun form "improving."
(3) This answer is plausible because a test taker who saw "to" as a preposition might feel that the object "improving" must have a parallel form following "and" ("making").
(4) This answer is plausible because a test taker may see that "the taking of" is similar to "to take." However, the infinitive "to take" is consistently used in the sentence, and the alternative shifts construction and is wordy.
(5) **This answer is correct as written.**

38.
(1) This answer is plausible because a test taker assumes that "having" is a verb and can be a subject's verb. However, "having" is a participle and would need a helping verb to be the verb for "nap."
(2) This answer is plausible because a test taker may not recognize that the independent clause/sentence is "the nap has long been" and sees "which has long been" as a subordinate/dependent clause describing "nap." In that case, the sentence does not have a verb.
(3) This answer is plausible because a test taker sees "long being" as a modifier for "nap." In that case, the sentence does not have a verb.
(4) This answer is plausible because a test taker may see "long been" as the verb for "nap." However, "been" is a past participle form and would require a helping verb to be the verb in the sentence.
(5) **This answer is correct because "the nap" is singular, requiring the singular verb "has."**

39.
(1) This answer is plausible because a test taker may think that "Because" makes the construction a fragment, consisting of a dependent/subordinate clause.
(2) **This answer is correct because "Because the midday sun makes it difficult to work" is an introductory adverb clause, so it must be followed by a comma.**
(3) This answer is plausible because a test taker may feel that "stores" should be possessive.
(4) This answer is plausible because a test taker may see a need to have a subject for the verb "close," and "they" would agree in number with "stores."
(5) This answer is plausible because a test taker may confuse the spelling of "meal" by spelling it phonetically.

40.
(1) This answer is plausible because a test taker may incorrectly see "planned rest" as the findings of "Using a variety of scientific methods."
(2) This answer is plausible because a test taker may see two actions ("using" and "discovering") as parallel in form.
(3) **This answer is correct because the introductory participial phrase must describe the noun which follows, and it is "researchers" who are "Using a variety of scientific methods."**
(4) This answer is plausible because a test taker may think that "they" worked "with researchers" in "Using a variety of scientific methods."
(5) This answer is plausible because a test taker may feel that what results from "Using a variety of scientific methods" is "benefits." However, it is not the benefits that are "Using a variety of scientific methods."

41.
(1) This answer is plausible because a test taker may possibly connect sentence 3 in paragraph A ("Some researchers believe . . .) with sentence 8's mention of "research findings."
(2) This answer is plausible because a test taker may feel that sentence 8's "research findings" should precede sentence 3's "researchers believe."
(3) This answer is plausible because a test taker may feel that sentence 8's "research findings" should follow sentence 3's "researchers believe."

- (4) This answer is plausible because a test taker may assume that sentence 5 presents the specific "research findings." Sentence 8 includes comments on sentence 5's content.
- **(5) This answer is correct because sentence 9 states the findings of the research. Sentence 8 states that "anyone who enjoys a nap" will not be "surprised" by the findings (in sentence 9).**

42.
- (1) This answer is plausible because a test taker may believe that adding an "s" to a verb makes it plural. "Research" is a singular noun requiring a singular verb.
- **(2) This answer is correct because verbs are made singular by adding an "s" to the ending of the verb.**
- (3) This answer is plausible because a test taker may assume that because the research had been conducted in the past, it needs a past tense verb.
- (4) This answer is plausible because a test taker may assume that research has been ongoing—initiated in the past and continuing into the present. Therefore, the present perfect tense would be needed.
- (5) This answer is plausible because a test taker may see the research continuing into the future before some additional future findings.

43.
- (1) This answer is plausible because a test taker may feel that the homophone "They're" is appropriate.
- (2) This answer is plausible because a test taker may not recognize that the possessive form "Their" is incorrect in this use.
- **(3) This answer is correct because the adverb "there" is an expletive used to get the inverted sentence (begins with "there" or "here") started. The subject of the verb "are" is "ways."**
- (4) This answer is plausible because a test taker may not understand that "ways," which is a plural noun, is the subject. The test taker may feel that "saving money" would be the singular subject.
- (5) This answer is plausible because a test taker may see the need for a possessive pronoun before "ways."

44.
- **(1) This answer is correct because it places the subject and verb at the beginning of the sentence. The modifying phrases describe parts at the end of the sentence.**
- (2) This answer is plausible because a test taker may read the revised sentence as "The cost (invested in energy savings) you will recover."
- (3) This answer is plausible because a test taker may relocate the introductory phrase "In energy savings" to the end of the sentence. The phrase should follow the verb "recover."
- (4) This answer is plausible because a test taker may feel that "of many times" will convey the lengthy return on "cost" savings.
- (5) This answer is plausible because a test taker read the revisions as increased "Energy" over the installation costs.

45.
- **(1) This answer is correct because the long gerund phrase "Installing . . . walls" is the subject of the verb "reduces."**
- (2) This answer is plausible because a test taker may feel that the underlined portion of the sentence explains the effect of "Installing insulating pads . . . ."
- (3) This answer is plausible because a test taker may see the construction "reducing the possibility of air leakage" as a participle describing the "walls" after the installation of the pads.
- (4) This answer is plausible because a test taker may see two independent clauses/sentences. One idea relates to installing insulating pads, and the second "Also greatly reduces air leakage."
- (5) This answer is plausible because a test taker may see two independent clauses/sentences. One idea relates to installing insulating pads, and the second to reducing air leakage.

46.
- (1) This answer is plausible because a test taker may see sentence 8 as a related idea for saving money by "add(ing) value to your home."
- (2) This answer is plausible because a test taker may see painting as a way to seal the cracks in one's home (sentence 6).
- (3) This answer is plausible because a test taker may see this sentence as transitioning from home energy savings to energy savings with the automobile.
- (4) This answer is plausible because a test taker may connect saving fuel with saving energy in the house.
- **(5) This answer is correct because the sentence has no relevance to the focus and details of the article.**

47.
- **(1) This answer is correct because the action of "idling" and "restarting" are occurring in the present time. Therefore, the present tense verb "uses" is needed.**
- (2) This answer is plausible because a test taker may feel that a subject (expletive "it") is needed for the verb "used." The test taker may be confused that "it," not "ten seconds," is the subject.
- (3) This answer is plausible because a test taker may confuse the close pronunciations of "then" and "than." However, "than" is needed because "idling" is being compared with "restarting."
- (4) This answer is plausible because a test taker may assume that since the past tense "used" precedes "restarting," the verbs must be parallel in tense.
- (5) This answer is plausible because a test taker may quickly read the sentence and assume the sentence "sounds" correct as written. However, the verb "used" must be in the present tense.

48.
- (1) This answer is plausible because a test taker may feel that the introductory phrase is too short and doesn't need a comma.
- (2) This answer is plausible because a test taker may confuse the homophone forms and choose the incorrect "wear."
- **(3) This answer is correct because a comma is needed to set off an introductory adverb clause ("where safety and conditions permit") from the subject and verb.**
- (4) This answer is plausible because a test taker may confuse the noun "half," which is needed as the object of the preposition "about," for the verb "halve."
- (5) This answer is plausible because a test taker may not realize that since "inch" begins with a vowel, "an" is the proper form of the article to use before a word beginning with a vowel.

49.
- (1) This answer is plausible because a test taker may assume that the verb's action occurred in the past.
- **(2) This answer is correct because "energy costs and pollution" are products of the automobile now, requiring the present tense of the verb.**
- (3) This answer is plausible because a test taker may think that "energy costs and pollution" are potential effects from the automobile and will occur in the future if action isn't taken now.
- (4) This answer is plausible because a test taker may see "contributing" as a participle describing the "automobile" and not see it as the verb.
- (5) This answer is plausible because a test taker may feel that the past perfect tense ("had contributed") is needed because the automobile was invented in the past and the results of "energy costs and pollution" also existed in the past, following the invention of the automobile.

50.
- (1) This answer is plausible because a test taker may misread the sentence so that "longer ones" and short "distances" are both objects of the verbs "walk or bicycle." As a result, the construction may be completed as "and longer ones for public transportation."
- (2) This answer is plausible because a test taker may feel that the subject "you" needs to be stated, and the subject and verb repeated after "distances."
- (3) This answer is plausible because a test taker may see "should" indicating a conditional action that "you" must take for traveling longer distances. However, the subject "you" (understood) would not agree with the verb "should be used."
- **(4) This answer is correct because the sentence is a compound sentence that contains two related independent clauses/sentences. (1) "Walk or bicycle short distances, and (2) for longer ones use public transportation." Since a comma is in place following "distances," all that is needed is the conjunction "and" to follow the comma.**
- (5) This answer is plausible because a test taker may confuse "longer use" for "longer distances."

Language Arts, Reading

*Exclusively provided and written by the GED Testing Service, answer explanations (rationales) for each test question are provided here for the Full-Length Official GED Practice Test.

1.
(1) This distractor is plausible because the excerpt describes Hancock's program as one that trains high school students to work in the hotel industry. However, the grant money is intended to pay compensation to the volunteers who work with the students.
(2) This distractor is plausible because the excerpt describes students who both work at Hancock and go to school. Test takers might assume that these buildings should be close to one another and that the grant money is intended to build a hotel with better proximity. However, the grant money is intended to pay compensation to the volunteers who work with the students.
(3) **This is the correct answer and can be found in lines 6–7 of the excerpt: "requesting $20,000 in federal grant money to compensate volunteers who work with their students."**
(4) This distractor is plausible because the excerpt mentions that the Hancock Training Program is available to students after school. However, the grant money is intended to pay compensation to the volunteers who work with the students.
(5) This distractor is plausible because the vocational program that is described in the excerpt refers to students who are both in school during the day and attend a work program in the afternoons. However, the grant money is intended to pay compensation to the volunteers who work with the students.

2.
(1) This distractor is plausible because the excerpt mentions that the Hancock students are in class in the morning and come to the hotel to work in the afternoon. However, students attend both high school and vocational training—not one or the other.
(2) This distractor is plausible because test takers may assume that, because the students are in the vocational hotel training program in addition to regular school, they will not graduate with other students in their class—perhaps because of their additional involvement with the Hancock program. However, the excerpt neither states nor implies this idea.
(3) This distractor is plausible because the excerpt mentions that students in the Hancock program learn to "establish an employment record" (line 31). However, the excerpt makes no mention of students having to maintain an employment record at their high schools as well.
(4) **This answer is correct because the excerpt (especially the section titled "Definition of the Program") describes in detail how the Hancock program trains young people who are also currently enrolled in high school.**
(5) This distractor is plausible because the excerpt mentions that the Hancock program is requesting a federal grant. However, the excerpt neither states nor implies that students who enroll in the program require federal approval to do so.

3.
(1) This distractor is plausible because people who give money often investigate the ability of the prospective grantee to manage and administer its programs. However, the additional information provided in this question suggests that Hancock actually has a proven record of success. It is illogical that this fact would then cause the funders to question Hancock's administration.
(2) This distractor is plausible because funders and people who make decisions about allocating money are often looking for worthy causes. However, the additional information provided in this question suggests that Hancock actually has a proven record of success in helping students get jobs. It is illogical that this fact would cause the decision-makers to look for a "worthier cause."
(3) **This answer is correct because the additional information provided in this question suggests that Hancock has a proven record of success in helping students get jobs. This record of success would cause the funders to look favorably on Hancock's proposal.**
(4) This distractor is plausible because decision-makers do have the power to deny Hancock's grant request. However, the additional information provided in this question suggests that Hancock actually has a proven record of success. It is illogical that this fact would then cause the decision-makers to deny the Hancock grant.
(5) This distractor is plausible because test takers may think that any transportation costs that are incurred by students going between school and the Hancock training facilities should be accounted for. However, the additional information provided in this question refers to Hancock's proven record of success. It is illogical that this fact would result in the inclusion of transportation costs in a budget.

4.
(1) This distractor is plausible because the excerpt is essentially a fundraising letter written by Hancock Training Center to decision-makers regarding the allocation of federal grant money. However, the students themselves are not involved in raising money and are not being taught these skills.
(2) This distractor is plausible because it may be necessary to operate heavy machinery in running a hotel (for example, landscaping or commercial laundry). However, lines 23–26 provide a detailed description of the skills that these students are learning, and this excerpt makes no mention of training that would help people operate heavy machinery.
(3) This distractor is plausible because high school students gain practice with research and writing, skills that would be useful as a journalist. However, these are not the types of skills that Hancock trains its students to do in the hotel management program.
(4) This distractor is plausible because test takers may connect the idea of raising money (and dealing with quantitative matters) with the teaching of math. However, lines 23–26 of the excerpt provide a detailed description of the skills that these students are learning

in the Hancock program, and none of them are related to instruction.

(5) **This is the correct answer. Lines 23–26 of the excerpt provide a detailed description of the skills that the students are learning in the Hancock program, and many of them are related to organization, preparation, scheduling—all important skills needed to run an office.**

5.
(1) This distractor is plausible because a test taker might think that Scratchy would be delighted to hear about Potter's marriage. However, the question refers to Scratchy's reaction to Potter's insistence that he doesn't have a gun, a fact that Scratchy finds hard to believe.
(2) This distractor is plausible because Potter appears to be indifferent in lines 29–30 to the threat of Scratchy's gun. However, the question refers to Scratchy's reaction to Potter's insistence that he doesn't have a gun, a fact that Scratchy actually finds hard to believe.
(3) This distractor is plausible because, in lines 50–52, Scratchy appears to be thoughtful as he considers the implications of Potter's marriage. However, the question refers to Scratchy's reaction to Potter's insistence that he doesn't have a gun, a fact that Scratchy actually finds hard to believe.
(4) **This is the correct answer. In lines 16–23, for example, Scratchy accuses Potter of lying when Potter tells him that he is carrying no gun.**
(5) This distractor is plausible because, in lines 50–63, Scratchy seems disappointed that Potter's marriage prevents Scratchy from continuing his aggressive challenge. However, the question refers to Scratchy's earlier reaction to Potter's insistence that he doesn't have a gun, a fact that Scratchy actually finds hard to believe.

6.
(1) This distractor is plausible if a test taker reads this description literally; sometimes when one is thirsty, one's throat can make such movements. Also, a test taker might assume that an "old Wild West" setting means that it is hot and dusty and that Scratchy must be thirsty. However, Scratchy is actually quite angry to hear that Potter is claiming to carry no gun. Earlier in that paragraph, the narrator describes Scratchy's face as "livid."
(2) **This is the correct answer. Scratchy is actually quite angry to hear that Potter is claiming to carry no gun. In line 16 of the excerpt, the narrator describes Scratchy's face as "livid," which means very angry.**
(3) This distractor is plausible if a test taker believes that Scratchy may be jealous of Potter's marriage. However, Scratchy is actually quite angry to hear that Potter is claiming to carry no gun. Earlier in that paragraph, the narrator describes Scratchy's face as "livid."
(4) This distractor is plausible if a test taker believes that Scratchy and Potter are actually friends and that Scratchy is simply teasing him.
(5) This distractor is plausible because Scratchy seems to be quite sincere about the intensity of his emotions. However, his specific emotion is one of anger at hearing that Potter is claiming to have no gun.

7.
(1) This distractor is plausible because a test taker might assume that, once Scratchy has accepted the fact of Potter's marriage, he feels that the matter is out of his hands and that he feels carefree. However, the excerpted line emphasizes the deep outline of Scratchy's boots in the heavy sand as he walks away; this image evokes a sense of heaviness, slowness, and disappointment.
(2) This distractor is plausible because a test taker might assume that Scratchy feels uncomfortable or nervous after hearing the unwelcome news of Potter's marriage. However, the excerpted line emphasizes the deep outline of Scratchy's boots in the heavy sand as he walks away; this image evokes a stronger sense of heaviness, slowness, and disappointment.
(3) This distractor is plausible because the test taker might assume that the news of Potter's marriage has left Scratchy feeling upbeat and optimistic. However, the excerpted line emphasizes the deep outline of Scratchy's boots in the heavy sand as he walks away; this image evokes a sense of heaviness, slowness, and disappointment.
(4) This distractor is plausible because the test taker might assume that the news of Potter's marriage has made Scratchy very happy for Potter.
(5) **This is the correct answer. The excerpted line emphasizes the deep outline of Scratchy's boots in the heavy sand as he walks away from Potter; this image evokes a sense of heaviness, slowness, and Potter's disappointment in the news about Potter's marriage.**

8.
(1) This distractor is plausible because the test taker might assume that the question is referring to Potter's feelings about his new wife. However, Scratchy's earlier violence in the story highlights the risk that Potter takes in refusing to fight him and also underscores Potter's courage in doing so.
(2) This distractor is plausible because the test taker might assume that Potter is inspired by his new wife to stand up to Scratchy. However, Scratchy's earlier violence in the story highlights the risk that Potter takes in refusing to fight him and also underscores Potter's courage in doing so.
(3) This distractor is plausible because the test taker might assume that Potter's actions are motivated by a new sense of forgiveness or generosity toward Scratchy. However, Scratchy's earlier violence in the story highlights the risk that Potter takes in refusing to fight him and also underscores Potter's courage in doing so.
(4) **This is the correct answer. Scratchy's earlier violence in the story highlights the risk that Potter takes in refusing to fight him and also underscores Potter's courage in standing his ground in front of this violent man.**
(5) This distractor is plausible because Scratchy does find Potter's actions to be disappointing. However, Scratchy's earlier violence in the story highlights the risk that Potter takes in refusing to fight him and also underscores Potter's courage in doing so.

9.
(1) This distractor is plausible because the test taker might assume that the townspeople would be more willing to accept the fact of Potter's marriage now rather than earlier because he's getting older. However, if Potter was worried that the townspeople would be concerned about his being married because they'd doubt his bravery, the fact that Potter defies Scratchy after his

marriage actually shows the townspeople that Potter's marital status has not diminished his courage.

- (2) This distractor is plausible because the test taker might assume that the townspeople would worry about the slowing effects of marriage on Potter. However, Potter's speed or slowness is not an issue, and the fact that Potter defies Scratchy after his marriage actually shows the townspeople that Potter's marital status has not diminished his courage.
- (3) This distractor is plausible because the townspeople might assume that Potter and his new wife might move elsewhere after their marriage to start a new life together. However, the encounter with Scratchy shows the townspeople that Potter's marital status has not diminished his courage.
- **(4) This is the correct answer. If Potter was worried that the townspeople would be concerned about his being married because they'd doubt his bravery, the fact that Potter defies Scratchy after his marriage actually shows the townspeople that Potter's marital status has not diminished his courage.**
- (5) This distractor is plausible because the test taker might assume that Potter is more easily prone to jealousy of other men after his marriage. However, the encounter with Scratchy shows the townspeople that Potter's marital status has not diminished his courage.

10.
- (1) This distractor is plausible because the excerpt describes a heated argument between Scratchy and Potter. However, the details of this dialogue in this excerpt most closely resemble a scenario where an athlete feels disappointed and frustrated that he will no longer have a rival against whom he can compete.
- (2) This distractor is plausible because the interaction between Scratchy and Potter resembles the intensity of arguing children. However, the details of this dialogue in this excerpt most closely resemble a scenario where an athlete feels disappointed and frustrated that he will no longer have a rival against whom he can compete.
- (3) This distractor is plausible because a test taker might assume that a business meeting might be a place where the participants argue with one another. However, the details of this dialogue in this excerpt most closely resemble a scenario where an athlete feels disappointed and frustrated that he will no longer have a rival against whom he can compete.
- **(4) This is the correct answer. The details of the dialogue between Scratchy and Potter in this excerpt most closely resemble a scenario where an athlete feels disappointed and frustrated that he will no longer have a rival against whom he can compete.**
- (5) This distractor is plausible because the test taker might assume that teachers using different materials to teach the same lesson might disagree with one another. However, the details of this dialogue in this excerpt most closely resemble a scenario where an athlete feels disappointed and frustrated that he will no longer have a rival against whom he can compete.

11.
- **(1) This is the correct answer. The speaker is referring to recreational activities that are defined by leisure, pleasure, fun, and relaxation.**
- (2) This distractor is plausible because the speaker refers to "phrases and meter" in line 5, which might cause the test taker to think of school and an educational context. However, the speaker is referring to activities that are defined by leisure, pleasure, fun, and relaxation.
- (3) This distractor is plausible because the test taker may think that the reference to "lyre" (line 13) reflects a prayerful or devotional context. However, in lines 9–11, the speaker is referring to activities that are defined by leisure, pleasure, fun, and relaxation.
- (4) This distractor is plausible because the idea of kidnapping might indicate that the poem's "you" (the reader) is in danger. However, the speaker is referring to activities that are defined by leisure, pleasure, fun, and relaxation.
- (5) This distractor is plausible because the test taker might notice the repetition of the phrase "if I were a poet I'd kidnap you" (lines 3–4 and lines 18–19) and assume that the activities reflect a habitual or repetitive context. However, in lines 9–11, the speaker is referring to activities that are defined by leisure, pleasure, fun, and relaxation.

12.
- (1) This distractor is plausible because the test taker might assume that, because line 3 is restated in line 18, the speaker is proud to be considered a potential poet. However, the question asks about the speaker's pride in the actual kidnapping; line 17 most closely reflects that sentiment in describing the speaker's wish to "show [the reader] off to mama."
- (2) This distractor is plausible because the speaker shows positive interest in including the reader in her "phrases and meter." However, the question asks about the speaker's pride in the actual kidnapping; line 17 most closely reflects that sentiment in describing the speaker's wish to "show [the reader] off to mama."
- (3) This distractor is plausible because line 8 suggests that the speaker would happily keep the reader at her house. However, the question asks about the speaker's pride (and not just a positive emotion) in the actual kidnapping; line 17 most closely reflects that sentiment in describing the speaker's wish to "show [the reader] off to mama."
- (4) This distractor is plausible because line 13 describes the speaker's happy willingness to play music for the reader. However, the question asks about the speaker's pride (and not just a positive emotion) in the actual kidnapping; line 17 most closely reflects that sentiment in describing the speaker's wish to "show [the reader] off to mama."
- **(5) This is the correct answer. The question asks about the speaker's pride in the actual kidnapping; line 17 most closely reflects that sentiment in describing the speaker's wish to "show [the reader] off to mama."**

13.
- (1) This distractor is plausible because a test taker might assume that stealing the reader's work is another example of a criminal activity—just like a kidnapping, which the speaker uses as a metaphor. However, the speaker uses the word "kidnap" to describe the effect she (as a poet) would like to have on a reader and his or her imagination.

- (2) **This is the correct answer. The speaker uses the word "kidnap" to describe the effect she (as a poet) would like to have on a reader and his or her imagination.**
- (3) This distractor is plausible because the speaker mentions the beach and a house in lines 6 and 7.
- (4) This distractor is plausible because the speaker lists several possibilities of actions she could take with a "kidnapped" reader; a test taker might assume that the reader can indicate likes and dislikes from this list. However, the speaker uses the word "kidnap" to describe the effect she (as a poet) would like to have on a reader and his or her imagination.
- (5) This distractor is plausible because kidnapping sometimes involves taking someone to another country. However, the speaker uses the word "kidnap" to describe the effect she (as a poet) would like to have on a reader and his or her imagination.

14.
- (1) This distractor is plausible because it mentions love, a word that also appears in line 14; however, the speaker makes no reference—stated or implied—to publication.
- (2) This distractor is plausible because it mentions "love poetry," which is closely linked to the definition of an ode. It also refers to music, and line 13 of the poem mentions a lyre, which is an ancient Greek instrument. However, the speaker makes no reference—stated or implied—to combining poetry and modern music.
- (3) **This is the correct answer. The speaker uses the word "ode" as a verb as a way of telling the reader that the speaker will place the reader at the center of a poem that is full of positive and strong emotions and images.**
- (4) This distractor is plausible because the test taker might assume from the question's introduction that the author has misused the word "ode." However, the speaker intentionally uses the word "ode" as a verb as a way of telling the reader that the speaker will place the reader at the center of a poem that is full of positive and strong emotions and images.
- (5) This distractor is plausible because the poem's metaphor—a kidnapping—can evoke a sense of the reader being held against his or her will by the kidnapper. However, the speaker intentionally uses the word "ode" as a verb as a way of telling the reader that the speaker will place the reader at the center of a poem that is full of positive and strong emotions and images.

15.
- (1) This distractor is plausible because the poet uses images and situations that are evocative of young and exuberant love. However, the poet's rejection of traditional grammar and punctuation suggests that she'd be most interested in writers who like to experiment and work beyond conventions.
- (2) This distractor is plausible because the poem's plot—a speaker's kidnapping of a reader into a poem—is unusual in the way that science fiction plots are often unconventional. However, the poet's rejection of traditional grammar and punctuation suggests that she'd be most interested in writers who like to experiment and work beyond conventions.
- (3) **This is the correct answer. The poet's rejection of traditional grammar and punctuation suggests that she'd be most interested in writers who like to experiment and work beyond conventions.**
- (4) This distractor is plausible because the speaker's reference to "phrases and meter" can imply an adherence to conventions and timeliness. However, the poet's rejection of traditional grammar and punctuation suggests that she'd be most interested in writers who like to experiment and work beyond conventions.
- (5) This distractor is plausible because this poem reflects the creativity and skill of a writer who is confident and is well known in her own right. However, the poet's rejection of traditional grammar and punctuation suggests that she'd be most interested in writers who like to experiment and work beyond conventions.

16.
- (1) This distractor is plausible because the meat pies are wrapped in newspapers. However, Annie is cooking fresh meat pies near the workers to attract them to her stall.
- (2) This distractor is plausible because many merchants might call out prices to attract shoppers. However, Annie is cooking fresh meat pies near the workers to attract them to her stall.
- (3) This distractor is plausible because the author mentions grease in line 7. However, Annie tries to get rid of the grease by wrapping the pies in newspaper. She cooks fresh meat pies near the workers to attract them to her stall.
- (4) **This is the correct answer. Annie is cooking fresh meat pies near the workers to attract them to her stall.**
- (5) This distractor is plausible because many merchants might use decoration to attract more shoppers to their stalls. However, Annie is cooking fresh meat pies near the workers to attract them to her stall.

17.
- (1) This distractor is plausible because merchants may price products according to their relative sizes. However, Annie sold leftover pies for 3 cents because they were leftovers and cold. The 5-cent pies cost more because they were fresh and hot.
- (2) This distractor is plausible because different variations of a product can have different prices. However, Annie sold leftover pies for 3 cents because they were leftovers and cold. The 5-cent pies cost more because they were fresh and hot. All of the pies were meat pies.
- (3) **This is the correct answer. Annie sold leftover pies for 3 cents because they were leftovers and cold. The 5-cent pies cost more because they were fresh and hot.**
- (4) This distractor is plausible because merchants will often vary their pricing, taking into account what different customers can afford. However, Annie sold pies at both prices to both the cotton gin and lumber mill workers. She sold some pies for 3 cents because they were leftovers and cold. The 5-cent pies cost more because they were fresh and hot.
- (5) This distractor is plausible because merchants might favor certain customers for a variety of reasons. However, Annie sold leftover pies for 3 cents because they were leftovers and cold. The 5-cent pies cost more because they were fresh and hot.

18.
- (1) This distractor is plausible because merchants will sometimes offer give-aways in order to strengthen their customer base. However, Annie charged all of her customers for the pies they bought. She initially ensured

the workers' loyalty to her product by regularly making and selling her pies in front of each factory.

(2) **This is the correct answer. Annie initially ensured the workers' loyalty to her product by regularly making and selling her pies in front of each factory before building a permanent stall some distance away.**

(3) This distractor is plausible because the excerpt mentions no other food vendor. However, Annie initially ensured the workers' loyalty to her product by regularly making and selling her pies in front of each factory before building a permanent stall some distance away.

(4) This distractor is plausible because the narrator mentions that cheese, meal, syrup, and cookies were later sold in a store that replaced Annie's stall. However, Annie initially ensured the workers' loyalty to her product by regularly making and selling her meat pies in front of each factory before building a permanent stall some distance away.

(5) This distractor is plausible because Annie locates her business in front of the lumber mill. However, she also locates it in front of the cotton gin—she alternates the days on which she arrives at each place first. She builds a permanent stall between these factories later.

19.
(1) **This is the correct answer. Over the course of the excerpt, Annie becomes a successful meat pie vendor and later a shop owner. In doing so, the narrator implies that Annie has taken a direction that is different from the one she'd earlier anticipated.**

(2) This distractor is plausible because Annie does regularly move between the cotton gin and lumber mill to sell her pies. However, the quotation refers to the narrator's implication that Annie's success as a vendor and shopkeeper has taken her down a different path in life than that she'd had earlier.

(3) This distractor is plausible because a test taker might assume that Annie sells different kinds of meat pies at different locations. However, she sells the same meat pies; the quotation refers to the narrator's implication that Annie's success as a vendor and shopkeeper has taken her down a different path in life than that she'd had earlier.

(4) This distractor is plausible because a test taker might assume that Annie's parents guided her actions and job choice. However, the excerpt makes no mention of her parents; the quotation refers to the narrator's implication that Annie's success as a vendor and shopkeeper has taken her down a different path in life than that she'd had earlier.

(5) This distractor is plausible because a test taker might interpret "the road" quite literally and assume that it refers to the trail or route that Annie takes every day to sell her meat pies. However, the quotation refers to the narrator's implication that Annie's success as a vendor and shopkeeper has taken her down a different path in life than that she'd had earlier.

20.
(1) **This is the correct answer. Annie's regular hard work to make fresh meat pies daily and sell them at two factories reflects her focus and determination to become a successful vendor.**

(2) This distractor is plausible because the test taker might assume that Annie would pray for help. However, this excerpt makes no mention of religion, faith, or prayer. Annie's regular hard work to make fresh meat pies daily and sell them at two factories reflects her focus and determination to become a successful vendor.

(3) This distractor is plausible because the excerpt mentions in lines 33–35 that Annie's future had "been chosen for her"; a test taker may assume that Annie is obedient. However, the description of Annie's regular hard work to make fresh meat pies daily and sell them at two factories reflects her focus and determination to become a successful vendor.

(4) This distractor is plausible because a test taker may assume that Annie is bitter about the hard work and long hours that she puts into making her business a success. However, the description of Annie's regular hard work to make fresh meat pies daily and sell them at two factories reflects her focus and determination to become a successful vendor.

(5) This distractor is plausible because a test taker may assume that Annie needs a sense of humor in order to put in all her hard work and long hours. However, the description of Annie's regular hard work to make fresh meat pies daily and sell them at two factories reflects her focus and determination to become a successful vendor.

21.
(1) This distractor is plausible because some students do fail to achieve in school because they put in little or no effort. However, the superintendent's letter focuses on changing the attitudes of students, parents, and teachers about students' ability to learn.

(2) This distractor is plausible because some teachers are reluctant to try new methods or include new material in their lessons. However, the superintendent's letter focuses on changing the attitudes of students, parents, and teachers about students' ability to learn.

(3) This distractor is plausible because many students have trouble in school because they have poor reading habits and skills. However, the superintendent's letter focuses on changing the attitudes of students, parents, and teachers about students' ability to learn.

(4) This distractor is plausible because many schools do need more qualified teachers than are readily available. However, the superintendent's letter focuses on changing the attitudes of students, parents, and teachers about students' ability to learn.

(5) **This is the correct answer. The superintendent's letter focuses on changing the attitudes of students, parents, and teachers about students' ability to learn. He describes research that finds a positive correlation between the level of expectations held for students and those students' achievement levels.**

22.
(1) This distractor is plausible because some test takers might believe that students would perform better in school if their teachers and parents were stricter. However, Mr. Hudson's metaphor of "raising the bar" suggests that an important way to increase student achievement is to challenge students by raising the academic standards and expectations to which they are held.

(2) This distractor is plausible because the metaphor that is used in this sentence is a sports reference. However, Mr. Hudson's metaphor of "raising the bar" suggests that

an important way to increase student achievement is to challenge students by raising the academic standards and expectations to which they are held.

(3) **This is the correct answer. Mr. Hudson's metaphor of "raising the bar" suggests that an important way to increase student achievement is to challenge students by raising the academic standards and expectations to which they are held.**

(4) This distractor is plausible because regular conversations about a student's performance might help his or her overall achievement level. However, Mr. Hudson's metaphor of "raising the bar" suggests that an important way to increase student achievement is to challenge students by raising the academic standards and expectations to which they are held.

(5) This distractor is plausible because a test taker might assume that, if a student sets his or her own goals, then his or her achievement level might be raised. However, Mr. Hudson's metaphor of "raising the bar" suggests that an important way to increase student achievement is to challenge students by raising the academic standards and expectations to which they are held.

23.
(1) This distractor is plausible because the inclusion of Dr. Resnick's quotations does make Mr. Hudson's letter longer. However, his primary goal in quoting her research is to provide an expert's perspective on the issue of higher expectations for students in order to support his main idea.

(2) This distractor is plausible because sometimes a writer will use quotes from someone else in order to present another viewpoint. However, Mr. Hudson and Dr. Resnick hold the same opinions regarding setting higher standards; his primary goal in quoting her research is to provide an expert's perspective on the issue of higher expectations for students in order to support his main idea.

(3) This distractor is plausible because sometimes when someone is quoted in an article or book, that person gains visibility with the public or colleagues. However, Dr. Resnick is already considered an expert in the field of student achievement. Mr. Hudson's primary goal in quoting her research is to provide an expert's perspective on the issue of higher expectations for students in order to support his main idea.

(4) This distractor is plausible because a test taker might assume that research or opinions given by experts might use confusing language or arguments. However, Mr. Hudson's primary goal in quoting Dr. Resnick's research is to provide an expert's perspective on the issue of higher expectations for students in order to support his main idea.

(5) **This is the correct answer. Mr. Hudson's primary goal in quoting Dr. Resnick's research is to provide an expert's perspective on the issue of higher expectations for students in order to support his main idea.**

24.
(1) This distractor is plausible because a test taker might assume that students would learn more from teachers who make them happy. However, Mr. Hudson's letter indicates his primary belief that teachers who hold students to higher standards would have the most impact on increasing student achievement.

(2) This distractor is plausible because a test taker might assume that students would learn best from teachers who give high grades. However, Mr. Hudson's letter indicates his primary belief that teachers who hold students to higher standards would have the most impact on increasing student achievement.

(3) This distractor is plausible because teachers who stay in touch with parents are often considered to be quite strong. However, Mr. Hudson's letter indicates his primary belief that teachers who hold students to higher standards would have the most impact on increasing student achievement.

(4) **This is the correct answer. Mr. Hudson's letter indicates his primary belief that teachers who hold students to higher standards would have the most impact on increasing student achievement.**

(5) This distractor is plausible because a test taker might assume that a teacher who is involved in community activities would help students learn. However, Mr. Hudson's letter indicates his primary belief that teachers who hold students to higher standards would have the most impact on increasing student achievement.

25.
(1) This distractor is plausible because the narrator describes the principal as a "remote silent man;" a test taker might assume that such a description would indicate that he does not get along with his teaching staff. However, the narrator explains in lines 21–22 that Helga knows the principal very little because Dr. Anderson was often away from the school on "publicity and money-making tours."

(2) This distractor is plausible because the narrator describes Helga's increasing "annoyance and discomfort" as she arrives at her appointment with the principal; a test taker might assume that Helga dislikes him. However, the narrator explains in lines 21–22 that Helga knows the principal very little because Dr. Anderson was often away from the school on "publicity and money-making tours."

(3) **This is the correct answer. The narrator explains in lines 21–22 that Helga knows the principal very little because Dr. Anderson was often away from the school on "publicity and money-making tours." These are responsibilities associated with his position as principal.**

(4) This distractor is plausible because the narrator describes the principal as someone who is busy with job-related traveling and meetings. However, the passage does not indicate that Dr. Anderson prefers others' company to Helga. In fact, the narrator explains in lines 21–22 that Helga knows the principal very little because Dr. Anderson was often away from the school on "publicity and money-making tours."

(5) This distractor is plausible because the excerpt reveals that Helga is unhappy in Naxos; therefore, a test taker might assume that Helga teaches in other places. However, the narrator explains in lines 21–22 that Helga knows the principal very little because Dr. Anderson was often away from the school on "publicity and money-making tours."

26.
(1) This distractor is plausible because Helga's anger toward the other teachers and about telling Dr.

Anderson about her resignation might indicate that she believes that these individuals are incompetent. However, in this excerpt, Helga begins to feel "an indistinct sense of sympathy" for Dr. Anderson, which then leads her to feel annoyed and angry at herself for caring about his reaction to the news of her resignation.
- (2) This distractor is plausible because the narrator describes Helga's emotions as she walks through the administration office (lines 45–54) as "outwardly indifferent." However, the people in this room are not people in authority.
- (3) This distractor is plausible because the narrator describes Helga as a strong character, one who will share her opinion of the other teachers with Dr. Anderson. However, in this excerpt, Helga begins to feel "an indistinct sense of sympathy" for Dr. Anderson, which then leads her to feel annoyed and angry at herself for caring about his reaction to the news of her resignation.
- (4) This distractor is plausible because a test taker might interpret Helga's strong emotions as confidence. However, she actually worries about others' reactions; in fact, in this excerpt, Helga begins to feel "an indistinct sense of sympathy" for Dr. Anderson, which then leads her to feel annoyed and angry at herself for caring about his reaction to the news of her resignation.
- (5) **This is the correct answer. In this excerpt, Helga begins to feel "an indistinct sense of sympathy" for Dr. Anderson, which then leads her to feel annoyed and angry at herself for caring about his reaction to the news of her resignation.**

27.
- (1) This distractor is plausible because a test taker might assume from the narrator's description of Helga's complex emotions that she feels uncomfortable because she's done something wrong. However, she is the one who requested the appointment with Dr. Anderson. Although she is uncomfortable with being at the center of attention (in the administration office), Helga forces herself to continue moving forward toward this important appointment in order to maintain her self-respect.
- (2) This distractor is plausible because it is possible that Dr. Anderson will be angry to hear that Helga is resigning. However, the question refers specifically to a scene in the administration office. Although she is uncomfortable with being at the center of attention (in the administration office), Helga forces herself to continue moving forward toward this important appointment in order to maintain her self-respect.
- (3) This distractor is plausible because a test taker might interpret Helga's mixed emotions as she approaches the office as an indication that she has decided not to resign and to continue in her current job. Although she is uncomfortable with being at the center of attention (in the administration office), Helga forces herself to continue moving forward toward this important appointment in order to maintain her self-respect.
- (4) **This is the correct answer. Although she is uncomfortable with being at the center of attention (in the administration office), Helga forces herself to continue moving forward toward this important appointment in order to maintain her pride and self-respect.**
- (5) This distractor is plausible because the narrator mentions that Helga likes and sympathizes with the principal. However, the question refers specifically to a scene in the administration office. Although she is uncomfortable with being at the center of attention (in the administration office), Helga forces herself to continue moving forward toward this important appointment in order to maintain her self-respect.

28.
- (1) **This is the correct answer. The stem of this question tells the reader that Helga notices the beauty of her natural environment while others around her do not. In addition, the narrator describes in the excerpt that Helga is highly attuned and sensitive to the feelings of others around her. These descriptions indicate Helga's perception of herself as particularly sensitive.**
- (2) This distractor is plausible because a test taker might assume that, because Helga teaches, she is more intelligent than others. However, the excerpt and the question's descriptions of Helga reflect her sensitivity to her surroundings and to the feelings of other people.
- (3) This distractor is plausible because Helga displays some sense of confusion in the excerpt's last scene as she enters the administrative office. However, the excerpt and the question's descriptions of Helga reflect her sensitivity to her surroundings and to the feelings of other people.
- (4) This distractor is plausible because a test taker might assume that Helga feels depressed about her treatment by the other teachers and her decision to resign from Naxos. However, the excerpt and the question's descriptions of Helga reflect her sensitivity to her surroundings and to the feelings of other people.
- (5) This distractor is plausible because the excerpt demonstrates Helga's determination in insisting on an appointment with Dr. Anderson. However, the excerpt and the question's descriptions of Helga reflect her sensitivity to her surroundings and to the feelings of other people.

29.
- (1) This distractor is plausible because a test taker might interpret Helga's change of mind regarding her job at Naxos as Helga's being able to laugh off and forget her earlier concerns about the other teachers. However, this decision to stay more reflects Helga's willingness to be flexible about her previous decisions and to not let her prior determination to leave Naxos sway her.
- (2) This distractor is plausible because Helga is described as being a strong and determined woman; a test taker might interpret this to mean that she doesn't listen to others' opinions. However, her decision to stay reflects Helga's willingness to be flexible about her previous decisions and to not let her prior determination to leave Naxos sway her.
- (3) This distractor is plausible because, as a teacher, Helga might often remember her own education as a student. However, her decision to stay more reflects Helga's willingness to be flexible about her previous decisions and to not let her prior determination to leave Naxos sway her.
- (4) **This is the correct answer. Her decision to stay more reflects Helga's willingness to be flexible**

about her previous decisions and to not let her prior determination to leave Naxos sway her.

(5) This distractor is plausible because the narrator describes Helga as a strong-willed woman. However, this decision to stay more reflects Helga's willingness to be flexible about her previous decisions and to not let her prior determination to leave Naxos sway her.

30.
(1) This distractor is plausible because a test taker might assume that Helga would be excited about leaving a principal whom she disliked intensely. However, based on Helga's reaction toward her current principal (for whom she feels an "indistinct sense of sympathy"), Helga would most likely feel justified and no regret in leaving someone so unpleasant.

(2) **This is the correct answer. Based on Helga's reaction toward her current principal (for whom she feels an "indistinct sense of sympathy"), Helga would most likely feel justified and no regret in leaving someone so unpleasant.**

(3) This distractor is plausible because the narrator describes Helga as "outwardly indifferent" in the excerpt. However, based on Helga's reaction toward her current principal (for whom she feels an "indistinct sense of sympathy"), Helga would most likely feel justified and no regret in leaving someone so unpleasant.

(4) This distractor is plausible because a test taker might assume that working with an unpleasant principal would be a depressing experience for Helga. However, based on Helga's reaction toward her current principal (for whom she feels an "indistinct sense of sympathy"), Helga would most likely feel justified and no regret in leaving someone so unpleasant.

(5) This distractor is plausible because a test taker might interpret the narrator's mention of Helga's "discomfort" (line 39) as embarrassment. However, based on Helga's reaction toward her current principal (for whom she feels an "indistinct sense of sympathy"), Helga would most likely feel justified and no regret in leaving another principal who was unpleasant.

31.
(1) This distractor is plausible because Andrew mentions "the home part" of living on a farm in line 5. However, Andrew is the brother who chooses to make the farm not only his home but also as a place "to work and grow things" (line 6).

(2) **This is the correct answer. Andrew is the brother who chooses to make the farm not only his home but also as a place "to work and grow things" (line 6). Even Robert describes Andrew as "wedded to the soil" (line 11).**

(3) This distractor is plausible because both of the brothers enjoy living on the farm. However, Andrew is the brother who chooses to make the farm not only his home but also as a place "to work and grow things" (line 6). Robert wants to travel and find his work elsewhere.

(4) This distractor is plausible because living and working on a farm is not really part of Robert's nature. However, the question asks about Andrew, who is the brother who chooses to make the farm not only his home but also as a place "to work and grow things" (line 6).

(5) This distractor is plausible because Robert mentions beauty and mystery in lines 64–75, and Andrew tells him that he can find everything he wants on the farm. However, Andrew is the brother who chooses to make the farm not only his home but also as a place "to work and grow things" (line 6). He loves the farm for reasons other than its beauty and mystery, which are the characteristics that Robert seeks.

32.
(1) **This is the correct answer. Andrew not only loves the farm as his home, but he also values it as his life's work. The welfare of the farm is always on his mind.**

(2) This distractor is plausible because the excerpt is entirely a conversation between two brothers who clearly care about each other. However, Andrew not only loves the farm as his home, but he also values it as his life's work. The welfare of the farm is always on his mind.

(3) This distractor is plausible because Robert mentions his and Andrew's father at the beginning of the excerpt.

(4) This distractor is plausible because a test taker might assume that a young man such as Andrew might spend much time thinking about his love life. However, the excerpt makes no mention of a girlfriend.

(5) This distractor is plausible because Andrew might well have to consider the wishes of his neighbors in certain decisions regarding the farm. However, the excerpt makes no explicit or implicit mention of neighbors. Instead, Andrew not only loves the farm as his home, but he also values it as his life's work. The welfare of the farm is always on his mind.

33.
(1) This distractor is plausible because Robert wants to leave the farm, and a test taker might assume that he feels angry about a lack of opportunities there. However, although Robert wishes to leave the farm to explore the world and have new experiences, he displays no anger in this conversation. Rather, he's looking for intangible elements of beauty and mystery. Andrew, on the other hand, finds his answers in the day-to-day workings of the farm.

(2) This distractor is plausible because a test taker might equate Robert's complex thought process with a tendency to work hard. However, Andrew clearly works hard on the farm himself. Robert is leaving in search of intangible elements of beauty and mystery. Andrew, on the other hand, finds his answers in the day-to-day workings of the farm.

(3) **This is the correct answer. Robert is leaving in search of intangible elements of beauty and mystery. Andrew, on the other hand, finds his answers in the day-to-day workings of the farm.**

(4) This distractor is plausible because Robert certainly does come across as thoughtful, sensitive, and mature. However, Andrew is also depicted this way—he cares very much for the welfare of the farm. Robert is leaving in search of intangible elements of beauty and mystery. Andrew, on the other hand, finds his answers in the day-to-day workings of the farm.

(5) This distractor is plausible because it is clear in this excerpt that Robert has made up his mind to leave the farm. However, Andrew is equally committed to his life on the farm and is decisive. Robert is leaving in search of intangible elements of beauty and mystery. Andrew, on the other hand, finds his answers in the day-to-day workings of the farm.

34.

(1) **This is the correct answer. The quoted lines in the question refer to humankind's quest to look for answers in unknown places that are beyond the boundaries and borders of familiar people and experiences.**

(2) This distractor is plausible because Andrew mentions the farm as "home" in the early part of the excerpt. However, the quoted lines in the question refer to Robert's—and humankind's—quest to look for answers in unknown places that are beyond the boundaries and borders of familiar people and experiences.

(3) This distractor is plausible because Andrew and his father seem to draw life from the soil (line 11: "wedded to the soil"). However, the quoted lines in the question refer to Robert's—and humankind's—quest to look for answers in unknown places that are beyond the boundaries and borders of familiar people and experiences.

(4) This distractor is plausible because many people do seek feelings of safety in their lives. However, the quoted lines in the question refer to Robert's—and many others'—quest to look for answers in unknown places that are beyond the boundaries and borders of familiar people and experiences.

(5) This distractor is plausible because many people do seek to create communities. However, the quoted lines in the question refer to Robert's—and humankind's—quest to look for answers in unknown places that are beyond the boundaries and borders of familiar people and experiences.

35.

(1) This distractor is plausible because clenched fists can indicate anger. Robert and Andrew have different opinions about what the farm means to them and what they are seeking in life. However, despite their differences, these brothers respect and love each other for who the other is. Putting an arm across each other's shoulders would indicate this affection and regard that they feel.

(2) This distractor is plausible because bowed heads can indicate silent disagreement. Robert and Andrew do have different opinions about what the farm means to them and what they are seeking in life. However, this excerpt shows that they do not have a problem with discussing it openly. Despite their differences, these brothers respect and love each other for who the other is. Putting an arm across each other's shoulders would indicate this affection and regard that they feel.

(3) This distractor is plausible because avoiding each other's eyes can indicate angry or embarrassed disagreement. Robert and Andrew do have different opinions about what the farm means to them and what they are seeking in life. However, this excerpt shows that they do not have a problem with discussing it openly. Despite their differences, these brothers respect and love each other for who the other is. Putting an arm across each other's shoulders would indicate this affection and regard that they feel.

(4) This distractor is plausible because leaving the stage in opposite directions can indicate fundamental disagreement and an unwillingness to understand another's viewpoint. Robert and Andrew do have different opinions about what the farm means to them and what they are seeking in life. However, this excerpt shows that they do not have a problem with discussing it openly. Despite their differences, these brothers respect and love each other for who the other is. Putting an arm across each other's shoulders would indicate this affection and regard that they feel.

(5) **This is the correct answer. Robert and Andrew have different opinions about what the farm means to them and what they are seeking in life. Despite their differences, these brothers respect and love each other for who the other is. Putting an arm across each other's shoulders would indicate this affection and regard that they feel.**

36.

(1) **This is the correct answer. A new mother speaks to her baby about its origins, its relationship to her, and the effects of the baby's arrival on the mother's life. Line 2 refers to "your bald cry"—a direct allusion to an infant's bald head, and line 10 mentions "your moth-breath" as a description of the baby's soft breathing.**

(2) This distractor is plausible because a test taker might assume that the speaker—a new mother—would tell the world about the significance of the arrival of her new baby. However, the speaker speaks to her baby about its origins, its relationship to her, and the effects of the baby's own arrival on the mother's life. Line 2 refers to "your bald cry"—a direct allusion to an infant's bald head, and line 10 mentions "your moth-breath" as a description of the baby's soft breathing.

(3) This distractor is plausible because a test taker might assume that the speaker—a new mother—would talk to the baby's father about the significance of the baby's arrival. However, the speaker talks to her baby about its origins, its relationship to her, and the effects of the baby's own arrival on the mother's life. Line 2 refers to "your bald cry"—a direct allusion to an infant's bald head, and line 10 mentions "your moth-breath" as a description of the baby's soft breathing.

(4) This distractor is plausible because the speaker may be mentioning family in line 6: "We stand round blankly as walls." However, the speaker talks directly to her baby about its origins, its relationship to her, and the effects of the baby's own arrival on the mother's life. Line 2 refers to "your bald cry"—a direct allusion to an infant's bald head, and line 10 mentions "your moth-breath" as a description of the baby's soft breathing.

(5) This distractor is plausible because this poem describes a mother's words. However, the speaker—a new mother--talks directly to her baby about its origins, its relationship to her, and the effects of the baby's own arrival on the mother's life. Line 2 refers to "your bald cry"—a direct allusion to an infant's bald head, and line 10 mentions "your moth-breath" as a description of the baby's soft breathing.

37.

(1) This distractor is plausible because as the wind blows at the cloud, the cloud becomes less whole and well-formed. A test taker might interpret this image as one where a mother becomes less attached to her child and loves it less. However, there is no indication in this

poem that the mother is worried about loving her child less. It is as time passes that the cloud loses its original shape; the image emphasizes more the passage of time.

(2) This distractor is plausible because as the wind blows at the cloud, the cloud becomes less whole and well-formed. It takes on other shapes, which might lead a test taker to interpret as learning new skills. However, it is as time passes that the cloud loses its original shape; the image emphasizes more the passage of time.

(3) This is the correct answer. As the wind blows at the cloud, the cloud becomes less whole and well-formed. It is as time passes that the cloud loses its original shape; the image emphasizes more the passage of time.

(4) This distractor is plausible because as the wind blows at the cloud, the cloud becomes less whole and well-formed. It takes on other shapes, which might lead a test taker to interpret as a mother's shifting of interest away from her child. However, it is as time passes that the cloud loses its original shape; the image emphasizes more the passage of time.

(5) This distractor is plausible because a test taker might assume that a mother's watching her child grow might remind her of her own childhood and friends. However, the quotation describes the ever-shifting shape of a cloud—much like the constant passage of time.

38.
(1) This is the correct answer. The speaker's description of the baby's breathing as "moth-breath" evokes a sense of a moth's lightness, softness, and quietness as it moves and lands in the darkness.

(2) This distractor is plausible because the speaker describes herself as "cow-heavy" in line 13. However, the speaker's description of the baby's breathing as "moth-breath" evokes a sense of a moth's lightness, softness, and quietness as it moves and lands in the darkness.

(3) This distractor is plausible because the speaker mentions the baby's "handful of notes" in line 17. However, the speaker's description of the baby's breathing as "moth-breath" evokes a sense of a moth's lightness, softness, and quietness as it moves and lands in the darkness.

(4) This distractor is plausible because the mention of the "pink roses" and "floral" nightgown can evoke a sense of cheeriness and brightness. However, the speaker's description of the baby's breathing as "moth-breath" evokes a sense of a moth's lightness, softness, and quietness as it moves and lands in the darkness.

(5) This distractor is plausible because a test taker might assume that a baby's breath can be congested and labored. However, the speaker's description of the baby's breathing as "moth-breath" evokes a sense of a moth's lightness, softness, and quietness as it moves and lands in the darkness.

39.
(1) This distractor is plausible because a test taker might assume that a child might call his or her mother when its sleep is disturbed. However, this child is actually an infant and can only cry. Line 13 starts with "One cry, and I stumble from the bed," which shows that the baby makes a single cry before the speaker—its mother—gets up to feed it.

(2) This is the correct answer. Line 13 starts with "One cry, and I stumble from the bed," which shows that the baby makes a single cry before the speaker—its mother—gets up to feed it.

(3) This distractor is plausible because a test taker might assume that when a child opens its eyes, the mother is ready to feed it. However, line 13 starts with "One cry, and I stumble from the bed," which shows that the baby makes a single cry before the speaker—its mother—gets up to feed it.

(4) This distractor is plausible because a test taker might assume that a child that hasn't cried at all might worry its mother. However, Line 13 starts with "One cry, and I stumble from the bed," which shows that the baby makes a single cry before the speaker—its mother—gets up to feed it.

(5) This distractor is plausible because many children might cry for several minutes before they are tended to. However, Line 13 starts with "One cry, and I stumble from the bed," which shows that the baby makes a single cry before the speaker—its mother—gets up to feed it.

40.
(1) This distractor is plausible because many poems rhyme. However, "Morning Song" does not contain a recognizable rhyme pattern. The additional information in the question helps to explain the speaker's thoughtful and complex reflections about her baby and her own role as a mother.

(2) This is the correct answer. The additional information in the question helps to explain the speaker's thoughtful and complex reflections about her baby and her own role as a mother.

(3) This distractor is plausible because a test taker might view the mention of the midwife as an example of the detail that Plath often includes in her poetry. However, the additional information in the question helps to explain the speaker's thoughtful and complex reflections about her baby and her own role as a mother.

(4) This distractor is plausible because a test taker might equate poetry about death with dark images. However, Plath's imagery in this poem is actually quite cheerful and optimistic (for example, "fat gold watch," "New statue," "pink roses," "clear vowels rise like balloons"). The additional information in the question helps to explain the speaker's thoughtful and complex reflections about her baby and her own role as a mother.

(5) This distractor is plausible because line 3 mentions "the elements," which a test taker might equate with natural landscapes. However, Plath sets this poem in a domestic setting with many images of manmade objects (for example, watch, museum, mirror, nightgown, wallpaper, window pane). The additional information in the question helps to explain the speaker's thoughtful and complex reflections about her baby and her own role as a mother.

Social Studies

*Exclusively provided and written by the GED Testing Service, answer explanations (rationales) for each test question are provided here for the Full-Length Official GED Practice Test.

1.
(1) This distractor is plausible if the test taker misread the table; however, based on the table, the supply of livestock products distinctly increased from 3.3 to 3.5 (7%). They did not decrease.
(2) This is the correct answer. The demand for soy is indicated in two places in the table, which together equal 40% increase.
(3) This distractor is plausible if the test taker misread the table; however, based on the table, the demand for tobacco products decreased, not increased: 1.6 down to 1.3 (–17%).
(4) This distractor is plausible if the test taker misread the table; however, based on the table, sugar products showed no change.
(5) This distractor is plausible if the test taker misread the table; however, based on the table, wheat products showed a decrease of –22%, not an increase.

2.
(1) This distractor is plausible because the excerpt states that all men are entitled to the right to pursue happiness; it does not state to what degree they should have these rights.
(2) This distractor is plausible because the excerpt states that all men are created equal and are able to have life, liberty, and happiness. There is no inclusion of economic concepts. Although one could argue that marginalized people do not have economic equality, the excerpt does not refer to this.
(3) This is the correct answer. The human rights referred to in the alternative translate to mean the equality, life, liberty, and happiness.
(4) This distractor is plausible because the excerpt states that all men are created equal; it does not mention women. However, this alternative is a judgment statement and is not based on the excerpt.
(5) This distractor is plausible because the excerpt mentions a creator. This excerpt is from the Declaration of Independence, not the U.S. Constitution/Supreme Court where church and state are more clearly defined.

3.
(1) This distractor is plausible if the test taker did not observe the evidence in the classroom. Based on the photograph and information, the U.S. flag hanging in the classroom shows allegiance to the United States; learning to speak English indicated they were not keeping the ways of their homeland—at least in school.
(2) This distractor is plausible if the test taker did not know about New York City. Based on the photograph, the picture was taken in New York City, clearly a big city—then and now.
(3) This distractor is plausible if the test taker did not understand the photograph or read the information carefully. The photograph and information clearly state that the children were learning the U.S. culture by learning English and saying the pledge.
(4) This distractor is plausible if the test taker made an assumption that people participate in a community just by living there. Based on the photograph and information, the children are in a big city, but there is no evidence provided about whether or not they participated in community affairs.
(5) This is the correct answer. Based on the photograph and information, children are clearly learning about the United States, which their parents encouraged them to do. This is what assimilation means.

4.
(1) This distractor is plausible if the test taker assumed going to the Colorado River must be fun. However, the map of the Colorado River Basin shows the geography of the area; if it is an enjoyable vacation area is a matter of opinion.
(2) This distractor is plausible if the test taker assumed rivers are polluted. The map of the Colorado River Basin shows the geography of the area. There is no evidence on the map to indicate it has become an ecological disaster. This is an opinion.
(3) This distractor is plausible if the test taker assumed there are always dams on rivers. Dams are not shown on the map, so having too many is an opinion.
(4) This is the correct answer. The map shows, as a fact, the cities to which the river basin supplies water.
(5) This distractor is plausible if the test taker assumed that the river basin is large and, thus, has a lot of water. The map only shows the distribution of the watershed, not the quantity of water. It is opinion whether or not the river basin has enough water to meet demands.

5.
(1) This distractor is plausible because Rachel Carson warned people of the dangers of pollution; however, this only indirectly relates to the question. The question asks about the slogan an environmental protection organization might use.
(2) This distractor is plausible if the test taker read the information about widespread use of pesticides and assumed people were out of control. Also, people are mentioned in the last part of the information, and a test taker might have keyed only into that word. Based on the information, Rachel Carson made no statement about being out of control; she warned of widespread damage to Earth. She did think people needed to take some responsibility for the preservation of the environment.
(3) This is the correct answer. Rachel Carson focused on Earth as it states in the stimulus. She believed that people are part of nature, and people should take responsibility for the environment.
(4) This distractor is plausible if the test taker assumed that technology can solve most problems. Rachel Carson does not mention technology in the information.
(5) This distractor is plausible if the test taker read about the use of DDT in the second paragraph, but did not read that the use of DDT causes damage. Based on the information, Rachel Carson told about the perils of DDT, not its usefulness.

6.
(1) This distractor is plausible if the test taker saw that horses were sent to the Americas and assumed they might be used in warfare. Based on the information and diagram, horse is mentioned as an animal sent to the Americas, but the diagram is about trade, not warfare.
(2) This is the correct answer. Based on the information and diagram, given the date of the Columbian Exchange, it can be inferred that Native Americans were receiving products, but the diagram also lists smallpox as a disease that was transported to the Americas.
(3) This distractor is plausible if the test taker assumed cultural exchanges occurred along with trade. This is often true; however, based on the information and diagram, the diagram is about trade, not religion.
(4) This distractor is plausible if the test taker misunderstood the direction in which the arrows were pointing on the diagram. Based on the information and diagram, corn and potatoes were sent overseas to eastern countries, not to the Americas.
(5) This distractor is plausible if the test taker assumed cultural exchanges occurred along with trade. This is often true; however, based on the information and diagram, the diagram is about trade, not the cultural aspects of the people doing the trading.

7.
(1) This distractor is plausible if the test taker observed the women working hard and assumed the conditions were safe. Based on the information and photograph, women are shown performing hard work, but there is nothing that indicates safer (or non-safe) working conditions.
(2) This distractor is plausible if the test taker thought women fought in wars, since women were sometimes near battle sites and now fly military jets. Women were not recruited for combat roles for WWII; the information at the top of the photo clearly states that the item refers to workers in 1943.
(3) This is the correct answer. When men went off to fight in WWII, women went to work in many factories to produce war-related items. This was a different role for women at this time.
(4) This distractor is plausible if the test taker thought Germany had more armament and supplies. Because women went to work in the factories, the United States continued to participate in the war. The information and photograph provide no evidence about Germany, but the workers produced materials for the military forces.
(5) This distractor is plausible if the test taker assumed the women were mostly working to produce goods for the home front. For the most part, factories were producing war-related products, and consumers were being asked to conserve certain items, turn in other items, and provided ration cards to get staples like sugar.

8.
(1) This is the correct answer. Based on the information, the rain forest is a fragile environment that is home to unique plants and animals that can only live in that location. These plants and animals provide humans with oxygen and useful medicines.
(2) This distractor is plausible if the test taker assumed that wood was harvested when the land was cleared for farming. The information does not mention wood products, and although it might be assumed that wood could come from the rain forest, this is not mentioned at the end of the passage where it indicates acres of land are being destroyed.
(3) This distractor is plausible if the test taker thought that clearing sites for factories would be more profitable. The information clearly indicates that cutting the rain forest is an unfortunate result of clearing land for ranching and farming.
(4) This distractor is plausible if the test taker thought that once the forest was cleared, people could move there and develop cities. The information clearly indicates that cutting the rain forest is an unfortunate result of clearing for ranching and farming; nowhere are cities mentioned.
(5) This distractor is plausible if the test taker might believe that tourists would like to visit rain forests to see all the plant and wildlife, but given the fragile nature of the rain forest, as mentioned in the passage, this type of activity would cause harm.

9.
(1) This distractor is plausible if the test taker honed in on only the words mentioned in the stimulus and neglected to read the words that negated the information. Cattle-ranching is mentioned in the information. However, the information mentions how devastating large-scale ranching is to the rain forest; more ranching does not provide the balance between economic and conservation efforts.
(2) This distractor is plausible if the test taker believes a compromise exists between the ranchers and fast-food chains. However, the information mentions how devastating large-scale ranching is to the rain forest. More ranching for beef does not provide the balance between economic and conservation efforts.
(3) This distractor is plausible if the test taker focused solely on the part of the stimulus that mentions preserving the tropical rainforests. The test taker might then have read the question and reversed what was actually being asked. Resettlement of city people to the rain forest (not taking people from cities to the rain forest) would cause more damage and does not provide the balance between economic and conservation efforts.
(4) This is the correct answer. This option shows the balance of the economic factor (limited farming) and the conservation factor (conserving the soil).
(5) This distractor is plausible if the test taker believes that resettlement and harvesting timber is a compromise. The test taker might believe people could make a better living in the city, so not as many people are needed to harvest timber. This alternative is the opposite of the question being asked. There is no balance of efforts if you move the native people out and destroy the rain forest with harvesting timber.

10.
(1) This is the correct answer. The information clearly indicates that the likes of U.S. citizens are different from those of French citizens. U.S. citizens will pay high prices and stand in lines, whereas the French people dislike this.
(2) This distractor is plausible if the test taker thought that only the French people visited the park; however, the first two paragraphs relate the issues the French had

with this amusement park. Based on the information, exchanges were taking place, but some of them needed to be reconsidered.
- (3) This distractor is plausible if the test taker does not think of Euro Disney as a product consumed by people. Consumers' tastes have much to do with a product's success. Consumers are the people buying the product or attending the attraction (which is a product also).
- (4) This distractor is plausible if the test taker believes this to be true about all individuals. Although some consumers' tastes may change quickly, the information does not tackle short-term changes in people's tastes. It is about a company that over time tried to accommodate people's tastes.
- (5) This distractor is plausible if the test taker thought that only the French people were having issues with the park. The information, however, concerns information that is important to a company.

11.
- (1) This distractor is plausible if the test taker reads the information that states that Euro Disney did hire local managers. However, the information states that hiring local French managers was positive, but the question asks what should be avoided.
- (2) This distractor is plausible if the test taker only recalled that the French are mentioned in the information. However, researching a group's preferences is also something Disney eventually did. In this question, the French could ask the Canadians their preferences. This is a positive outcome, whereas the question asks what should be avoided.
- **(3) This is the correct answer. Because the question was worded in the negative, the reader should have interpreted the word *avoid* as something to stay away from. The information stated that a negative aspect of Euro Disney was that the high cost of tickets kept many people away. If a French company is opening a business to sell products, then it would want to avoid charging prices people could not afford.**
- (4) This distractor is plausible if the test taker does not understand that a temperate climate is one that is comfortable most of the time. The temperate climate of Florida helped Disney. The French company would want to investigate a good location for its company. This is a positive outcome, whereas the question asks what should be avoided.
- (5) This distractor is plausible if the test taker misinterpreted the word *avoid*. When an item is worded in the negative, it can be difficult for the test taker to remember that he or she is looking for something that is not a good idea. In this case, the last line of the stimulus states that new advertising campaigns helped to point out the positive aspects of Euro Disney. A new company would want to advertise its products so that consumers want to purchase the product.

12.
- (1) This distractor is plausible if the test taker believed that all people are civilized, but particularly all men. Although the excerpt mentions that it is a right most valued by civilized men, the alternative provides an opinion that only civilized men enjoy the right to privacy. Uncivilized men and women in the U.S. have this right also.

- **(2) This is the correct answer. The Supreme Court ruling makes it appear that it is a basic right covered in the Bill of Rights. Though not stated in those exact words, the Supreme Court interprets the Constitution.**
- (3) This distractor is plausible if the test taker was unaware that when a case is against the United States, it is an issue with the Constitution. The Supreme Court has the power to hear any cases that involve constitutionality.
- (4) This distractor is plausible if the test taker might believe this from personal experience. The test taker may believe that most people do not get involved for a common cause. There is no indication in the excerpt that civilized men want to be left alone, but they do have that right.
- (5) This distractor is plausible if the test taker believed that the Founding Fathers did not believe in the right to privacy because it is not addressed outright in the Constitution. The right to privacy was not confirmed as a right until much later when the Bill of Rights was adopted. The Supreme Court interpreted this right in the *Olmstead* case in 1928.

13.
- (1) This distractor is plausible if the test taker believes that a limited government is best. The test taker might also interpret the cartoon incorrectly because all the people were in a straight line toward one goal. Having the right to vote does not necessarily mean the government is limited or is not limited. The cartoon only illustrated the right to vote.
- (2) This distractor is plausible if the test taker does not understand the meaning of the rule of law. The rule of law implies that government authority may be only exercised in accordance with written laws, which are generally outlined in democratic constitutions. If a government holds free and open elections, then voting would be in support of the rule of law. Thus, the rule of law would not be suspended.
- (3) This distractor is plausible if the test taker believes this to be true. Some individuals may feel that giving up certain rights is better than people breaking the law. The cartoon addresses only the ability to change government through voting.
- **(4) This is the correct answer. The large hand with the broken chain indicates that the people are now free to vote and to choose the people they want to be in charge of government. For many years in South Africa, black individuals were treated as second-class citizens and were not afforded the same rights as white South Africans, including the right to vote.**
- (5) This distractor is plausible if the test taker believes that the only way to make true change is through violent and public means. The cartoon addresses only the ability to change government through voting. There is nothing in the cartoon that indicates a violent revolution is taking place.

14.
- **(1) This is the correct answer. Based on the information, a representative democracy allows free elections that can change the political climate. Communism does not allow this.**
- (2) This distractor is plausible if the test taker thinks a representative democracy is only about voting, Congress, and the president. Based on the information, the topic is

about the differences between voting in a representative democracy and in a Communist state. To the contrary, the U.S. government is involved in the economy.
- (3) This distractor is plausible if the test taker confused the two systems and did not recall the checks and balances that operate in the U.S. government. Based on the information, the opposite is true. Communist countries have one party, and representative democracies, by their very name, have multiple parties.
- (4) This distractor is plausible if the test taker remembers that there is only one party in the Communist system, and therefore, the citizens do not vote. Based on the information, one part of this alternative is true. In representative democracies, people have the right to vote. However, the second part of the alternative is false. Citizens in Communist states can vote, but it is limited to one party.
- (5) This distractor is plausible if the test taker confuses the difference between political parties in the two systems. Based on the information, this alternative is opposite to the one above. In a representative democracy, political parties can make a difference in government; in a Communist state, the party is all-powerful.

15.
- (1) This distractor is plausible if the test taker sees this system as unfair and only settled in a court of law. Based on the information about sharecropping, there is no mention of any court trials or fairness before the courts.
- (2) This distractor is plausible if the test taker believed that sharecropping was good for the owner of the land and did not read the question carefully; the question is based on the African American viewpoint. Based on the information about sharecropping, this type of work returned little on the investment of hard work and low farm prices. They barely made enough money to provide the necessities and often owed money for things purchased on credit.
- (3) This distractor is plausible if the test taker believed that since the sharecroppers lived on someone else's land, they had no other ties. Most sharecroppers were African Americans and white people from the South, as stated in the information. They were strongly tied culturally and socially through family and church.
- (4) This distractor is plausible if the test taker read the information about the ability of sharecroppers to leave the state but missed the part about paying debts. Based on the information, the sharecroppers could move as long as they did not owe money.
- **(5) This is the correct answer. Even with the Emancipation Proclamation and Amendments 13, 14, and 15, African Americans were not accepted into mainstream white society, so their economic choices were few.**

16.
- (1) This distractor is plausible if the test taker thought if the sharecropper gave the landlord enough money, eventually the sharecropper would own the land. Based on the information, sharecroppers only worked the land for a landlord and kept only a portion of the earnings while the rest went to the landlord. They could never own the land.
- (2) This distractor is plausible if the test taker focused only on the low wages. However, this was only part of a larger problem of debt. Even though low wages would be a hindrance, economic independence could eventually have been achieved. However, as test takers continue to analyze the options, they would discover in the stimulus that sharecroppers often bought supplies on credit. When the harvest was sold and the sharecropper got his share, he had to pay creditors. He often didn't earn enough money to pay his debt.
- (3) This distractor is plausible if the test taker believed that only the landlord benefited from a crop surplus. Based on the information, sharecroppers rarely had surplus crops. There often were times of poor harvests and low crop prices.
- **(4) This is the correct answer. Based on the information, sharecroppers often found themselves in financial debt. They owed money to the landlord or to merchants. It was difficult to get ahead in order to gain financial independence.**
- (5) This distractor is plausible if the test taker thought the sharecroppers were still enslaved directly or indirectly by owing their livelihoods to a landlord. By this time in history, the African Americans were free to move anywhere as long as they did not owe money as a sharecropper.

17.
- (1) This distractor is plausible if the test taker thought the civil rights movement was occurring at this time, although the dates are listed in the reading (1875–1900). Based on the information, the Tuskegee Institute provided education. There is no direct indication that the institute was involved in outward civil rights support.
- **(2) This is the correct answer. Based on the information, the Tuskegee Institute provided educational opportunities to African Americans with the hope that with skills, they could raise their income and get better treatment.**
- (3) This distractor is plausible if the test taker remembered that African Americans were often segregated from white institutions, transportation, schools, etc. However, the Tuskegee Institute was designed for African Americans. Because no other ethnicities went to the institute at the time, racial segregation did not occur.
- (4) This distractor is plausible if the test taker thought that African Americans could not move to urban areas because of segregation. Although being accepted into urban areas might have been a problem in some areas, many African American populated the inner cities. Based on the information, this was not the primary goal.
- (5) This distractor is plausible if the test taker believed an education provided mobility to other areas of the country. Although moving to either the North or West could have been a byproduct of attending the institute, based on the information, it was not the primary goal.

18.
- **(1) This is the correct answer. Based on the information, laws about sharecropping served to keep African Americans from owning land. It was believed that owning land would provide a higher economic status for the African Americans and that they would desire more equality. Many people at the time did not have high regard for African Americans.**

(2) This distractor is plausible if the test taker thought about the amendments that gave freedoms to African Americans. Based on the information, sharecroppers were not free to move if they owed money, and most did not earn enough money from the sale of their crops, especially after paying the landlord and any other debts. Besides, many individuals did not want the African Americans to gain economic freedom because of added economic competition and beliefs that they were different.
(3) This distractor is plausible if the test taker saw the word *discouraged* and believed that this alternative was negative, and thus, untrue. At this time in history, cotton and tobacco were the cash crops the South depended on, as stated in the information. Later farming practices showed that rotating crops was beneficial.
(4) This distractor is plausible if the test taker assumed that the Northern Radical Republicans had authority over laws and practices. Based on the information, there was no mention of this particular political party or any other party. The only law mentioned was the one that forbid sharecroppers to move unless all debts were paid.
(5) This distractor is plausible if the test taker believed the laws about sharecroppers were written into the U.S. Constitution. The information did not mention the U.S. Constitution, and it includes no such federal laws. If there were such a law, it would most likely be passed by an individual state. Not all states had sharecroppers.

19.
(1) This distractor is plausible if the test taker did not understand the term *primary source*. Because the word *book* is mentioned in this alternative, there is evidence of a written language that would not be considered prehistoric.
(2) **This is the correct answer. To answer the question, the definition of primary source is important: it is the basis of information that is seen first-hand and recorded, a genuine relic made by the original people, or the telling of an event by the person who experienced it. A stone tool made by a Neanderthal is prehistoric (before writing).**
(3) This distractor is plausible if the test taker believed painting came before writing. A painting might be a primary source, but in this case, there is no indication when the painting was produced, but it is stated that the painting is of someone from the Renaissance. Writing was invented by the time of the Renaissance.
(4) This distractor is plausible if the test taker did not know when writing was invented. There was writing during the ancient Greek period.
(5) This distractor is plausible if the test taker did not know when writing was invented. There was writing during the time of ancient Rome.

20.
(1) This distractor is plausible if the test taker believed that separating groups would lead to less conflict. Based on the information, globalization is a good way to bring groups together rather than separate them.
(2) This distractor is plausible if the test taker believed military action is the only way to end conflicts. The information talks about ending conflict. A more effective military force would cost money that many of these regions do not have, and it might actually incite more conflict.
(3) This distractor is plausible if the test taker believed imprisoning the government opposers would cause less conflict. Although imprisoning these people might give the impression that conflicts would be reduced, based on the information, it is better to provide people with a good income through economic globalization.
(4) This distractor is plausible if the test taker believed freedom of speech and religious freedom caused ethnic conflicts. Some test takers may come from countries that have religious or ethnic conflicts. Limiting human or civil rights tends to create conflict. In order to create prosperity, people need economic stability.
(5) **This is the correct answer. Based on the information, new trading partners would contribute to economic globalization and reduce ethnic conflicts.**

21.
(1) This distractor is plausible if the test taker had this opinion. Based on the graph, there is no separation of gender. There is no way of knowing who voted in greater numbers.
(2) This distractor is plausible if the test taker equated numbers of voters with the number of candidates running for office. Even though this is a graph about presidential elections, there is no indication how many candidates had run for president.
(3) **This is the correct answer. The graph indicates a gradual decline in the percentage of those voting in presidential elections from 1876 to 1920 (81.8% down to 49.2%).**
(4) This distractor is plausible if the test taker had this opinion. Based on the graph, there is no information about the difference between middle class and wealthy voters to know who voted in greater numbers.
(5) This distractor is plausible if the test taker assumed that fewer people voted because fewer people qualified to vote. There is no mention of voting qualifications.

22.
(1) This distractor is plausible if the test taker interprets the trend line as positive for growth. However, the graph shows that by the second year, 25% of the new businesses fail. Because the stimulus tells the reader that an entrepreneur is a person who starts new businesses, the test taker needs to apply that knowledge to the question. The graph indicates that entrepreneurs are more likely to fail as the trend line climbs over the years.
(2) This distractor is plausible if the test taker is unsure what conservative means, or doesn't understand the risk involved with entrepreneurship. Entrepreneurs are those who are willing to take a risk by creating something new, rather than working at an established job.
(3) This distractor is plausible if the test taker interprets the trend line as positive for growth. Based on the graph, 25% fail within two years, and in eight years, 75% fail. There is no way to tell from this graph which specific businesses fail and which ones succeed. The graph shows only the number of business failures over time. The title and labels on the graph directly state there are going to be business failures.
(4) This distractor is plausible if the test taker believes that all entrepreneurs hire managers to do the everyday business of running a company or business. Based on the information, entrepreneurs invest their own

time and money to create a new business. There is no mention of entrepreneurs relying on anyone to manage the businesses.
- **(5) This is the correct answer. By the nature of being an entrepreneur, the ability to sense the needs of the marketplace and to anticipate demands is a risky undertaking. It is also risky to strike out on your own with just your own idea; you could invest all your money and have the business fail.**

23.
(1) This distractor is plausible if the test taker believed taxes are necessary, but because the taxes are spread over eight years, the impact is acceptable. An increase in business taxes would only hurt the entrepreneur who needs cash to put into the business.
- **(2) This is the correct answer. The government could help best by finding ways to slow the failure rate. This could mean tax breaks, for example.**
(3) This distractor is plausible if the test taker interpreted the word *stop* as a way to help businesses succeed. The test taker might think that putting money into research was wasteful when the businesses needed the money to continue operating. The government could help entrepreneurs by continuing to study the reasons for failure and to find ways to prevent the failures.
(4) This distractor is plausible if the test taker believed that fewer choices would help the entrepreneur get a better start. The basis for a capitalistic society such as the United States depends on competition to drive down prices. An entrepreneur would benefit by providing another choice for consumers.
(5) This distractor is plausible if the test taker believed that the information in the graph would not help people in the real world. On the contrary, it is to the to consumers' benefit and the overall economy for the government to help entrepreneurs to succeed. If the government can identify what is causing the downward trend, it can help prevent future business failures.

24.
(1) This distractor is plausible if the test taker believed that education provides the means to develop technology. The information includes the ability of Western Europe to harness science and technology. Although some of this knowledge may have had its roots in universities, the alternative addresses the technical advantage. Building universities does not address the question.
(2) This distractor is plausible if the test taker believed that the development of metals helped build armies. However, the type of military units used in battle are not based on the technical advantages of a nation. The types of troops used depend on the requirements of the military action.
(3) This distractor is plausible if the test taker believed airplanes existed during this time period. Airplanes were not available at this time. Their real use in battle didn't occur until WWI.
- **(4) This is the correct answer. Based on the information, metals that were stronger and more useful were developed through better science and technology, so Europeans could produce more effective weapons of war.**

(5) This distractor is plausible if the test taker believed the technological advances helped in medical research. The information does not mention medical research. Although indirectly science and technology might help this field, it would not lead to a power shift to Europe.

25.
- **(1) This is the correct answer. Using the key to the map, the partly-free countries together with the not-free countries provide evidence that governments did not protect personal freedoms.**
(2) This distractor is plausible if the test taker misinterpreted the question and believed it was non-democratic countries that had weak military forces. The question asks about freedom, not military forces. There are plenty of democratic countries with few military resources and plenty of non-democratic countries with large military forces.
(3) This distractor is plausible if the test taker misinterpreted the map and viewed the partly-free and the non-free countries as decreasing compared to the free countries. There is no way to tell from this map whether there has been a decrease in democratic countries. The question asks about democratic freedoms only.
(4) This distractor is plausible if the test taker assumed that because there are many democratic countries, they all had free elections. There is no way to tell from this map whether free elections took place in most countries. The question asks about democratic freedoms only. The inclusion of *free elections in most countries* makes the question too broad. Democratic and non-democratic countries might have free elections.
(5) This distractor is plausible if the test taker assumed that all democratic countries protect freedom of the press. There is no way to tell from this map whether most governments protected freedom of the press. The question asks about democratic freedoms only. The inclusion of *most governments* makes the question too broad. Democratic and non-democratic countries might have freedom of the press.

26.
(1) This distractor is plausible if the test taker was unaware of the correct meaning of civil rights. Based on the photograph and information, the civil rights movement is incorrect because the photograph concerns a bird and because there are no people protesting for equal opportunity.
(2) This distractor is plausible if the test taker believed that anti-war was meant in a generic way—such as a war with people and the environment. Based on the photograph and information, there is no indication that the man and the bird are involved in an anti-war movement.
(3) This distractor is plausible if the test taker interpreted the photograph as showing only a man instead of a woman in what appears to be a scientific job. Based on the photograph and information, there is no indication that the man and the bird are involved in the women's rights movement or that any woman or women's rights group are involved with the situation shown in the photograph. The focus in the photograph is what the man is doing to help the bird contaminated through an oil spill.

- (4) **This is the correct answer. This analysis question requires a test taker to analyze the photograph to grasp what it means for a worker in gloves and work overalls to be cleaning a bird drenched in oil. Also, the information gives clues about an oil tanker and its effects on wildlife.**
- (5) This distractor is plausible if the test taker believed the photograph concerned the working conditions of the man. Based on the photograph and information, because the man is cleaning the bird, there is no indication that he belongs to a union or not; he could be a volunteer. The consequences of the incident are about the bird, not the labor involved in helping the bird.

27.
- (1) **This is the correct answer. Based on the information, both governments provide aid for children. The governments must feel this is their responsibility or they wouldn't set aside funding.**
- (2) This distractor is plausible if the test taker believed that there are too many tax-based programs already. Based on the information, the governments are using tax dollars to fund these programs; whether or not tax dollars should be spent is a matter of opinion.
- (3) This distractor is plausible if the test taker thought that parents did not put the money to wise use to help their children. Children (the program concerns those 5-years-of-age and younger) are not able to spend money wisely, so the money is given to the parents with the hope that they will spend the money wisely.
- (4) This distractor is plausible if the test taker believed this was true, especially if the test taker had experience with older children. There is no indication in the information that discusses whether older children need more assistance.
- (5) This distractor is plausible if the test taker believes little children are unaware of poverty. These children may not be able to express what poverty is, but they are affected as are their parents (money, food, education, and housing to name a few). If children were not affected, this type of program and other government-funded aid programs would not exist.

28.
- (1) This distractor is plausible if the test taker believed the Greeks did more than what is mentioned in the information. Based on the information, the wheel and gunpowder are not mentioned. China is given credit for the invention of gunpowder around 100 B.C. The invention of the wheel came much earlier than gunpowder, but there are differences of opinion about who invented it.
- (2) **This is the correct answer. Based on the information, fitness and health are mentioned as well as the form of government that allows males to participate. This infers that the Olympic Games contribute to fitness and that their type of government refers to democracy.**
- (3) This distractor is plausible if the test taker was unaware of when these three items were produced. Based on the information, the Bible, hieroglyphics, and the abacus are not mentioned, and there is nothing provided in the information where these could be inferred. The Bible was translated after the ancient Greek civilization, hieroglyphics were used much earlier than the ancient Greeks, and the abacus can be dated back as far as the Babylonians and Egyptians.
- (4) This distractor is plausible if the test taker knew these two religions were old. Based on the information, Greeks had many gods they worshipped, but Buddhism and Hinduism are not mentioned.
- (5) This distractor is plausible if the test taker knew that the Greeks had classical architecture. Based on the information, architecture and Christianity are not mentioned. The ancient Greeks did have unique architecture, but Christianity came about much later.

29.
- (1) This distractor is plausible if the test taker assumes the camera store is a business, and therefore, has a business plan. Based on the advertisement, there are only pictures of cameras with their prices. Although it is the company's plan to sell inexpensive cameras, a business plan is a formal strategy for running an entire business, including the budget, employees, etc.
- (2) This distractor is plausible if the test taker assumed the sign next to the Focus Camera sign meant the store was for sale, or the test taker read too quickly and missed an important piece of information. Based on the advertisement, no mention of someone buying the entire store as a whole is mentioned. The reference is for individuals to buy cameras. Even if someone bought all the cameras at one time, the store would replenish the inventory.
- (3) This distractor is plausible if the test taker determined that because there was a sale, many buyers would come to the store, so more people needed to be hired. Based on the advertisement, there is no mention of new employees. There would most likely be a separate advertisement, or at the very least, a clear message on this advertisement.
- (4) **This is the correct answer. The advertisement shows reduced prices, which would entice a consumer. The fine print at the bottom of the advertisement refers directly to people who purchase the camera.**
- (5) This distractor is plausible if the test taker assumed that when a product is purchased, a sales person shows how to use the product. Based on the advertisement, only the sale discounts are mentioned. Often a product comes packaged with directions. The advertisement does not indicate instructions.

30.
- (1) This distractor is plausible if the test taker did not read the form carefully and only saw that the form had good organization. Based on the form, the questions that are asked do not relate to organizing a business.
- (2) This distractor is plausible if the test taker only read the portion of the form that asks for personal information and references. Based on the form, the title does not indicate a job opening and no questions ask about work experience.
- (3) **This is the correct answer. The form title is Credit Application. A form of this nature is used to borrow money. The questions ask for information about income and how much money is to be borrowed.**
- (4) This distractor is plausible if the test taker only read the bottom of the forms that asks about income. The form title does not refer to taxes. On a tax form, the amount of money earned and the amount of money paid in taxes is required.

(5) This distractor is plausible if the test taker read about the money request. The form title refers to credit, and the form asks about how much money is requested. It does not indicate that money needs to be exchanged into other currency.

31.
(1) This distractor is plausible if the test taker did not read carefully enough. Based on the form, a person would not need money to give away a car; it is free.
(2) This distractor is plausible if the test taker did not read carefully enough. Based on the form, a person would not need a loan to wash a car because it is a relatively inexpensive activity. Loans are usually for large quantities of money.
(3) This distractor is plausible if the test taker equated buying a car with driving a car. There is no need for a loan to drive a car. Gas may be expensive, but a person would typically not need a loan for this purchase.
(4) This distractor is plausible if the test taker thought in terms of the car company selling a car, in which case an individual would need a loan. Based on the form, the request is for credit. Selling a car gives the seller money. A loan gives the buyer money.
(5) This is the correct answer. Because a car is often purchased over time instead of with cash at the time of purchase, a credit application might be required to check a person's credit. The car company wants to know that the loan will be repaid.

32.
(1) This distractor is plausible if the test taker believed the factory had serious problems that would affect its ability to continue business. The safety policies of a company would be a concern only to the company that has the problems. Applicants would be unaware of these policies.
(2) This is the correct answer. Loans typically have a certain rate of interest that is charged in addition to the actual loan. The interest rate is sometimes based on the amount of money or the credit rating of the individual. If interest rates are high, people generally don't buy things like houses or cars. When the interest rates are low, people tend to buy expensive items for which they need a loan. If a company was losing customers, the company would check other companies' interest rates. In order to compete for more applicants, the company may want to adjust their interest rate.
(3) This distractor is plausible if the test taker believed that asking for ID violated individual rights to privacy. Photo identification is usually required by all loan companies when a person applies for a loan. This is to prevent fraud.
(4) This distractor is plausible if the test taker believed that more people are traveling by air and don't need as many new cars. If there was a decline in loans, air travel would not be the cause. People may borrow money if they are taking expensive trips, but this would not cause a decline in business.
(5) This distractor is plausible if the test taker believed that this would be a frustration for the borrower. Based on this form, only one reference is required. There is no way of knowing if adding one, two, or five more requests for references would decrease loan applications.

33.
(1) This distractor is plausible if the test taker determined that the best wildlife protection would be to fence in the wildlife. Based on the information, having confined urban areas allows for more open space so wildlife can be protected while roaming free.
(2) This distractor is plausible if the test taker thought that the main idea of the information was to spread out from the cities, which would require more roads. Based on the information, more paved roads encourages people to spread out. When people are spread out and develop lands, available drinking water is negatively impacted.
(3) This is the correct answer. Based on the information, urban centers are more economically practical and government agencies can provide better services.
(4) This distractor is plausible if the test taker believed that being in an urban center would mean less distances to travel; therefore, driving would be economically feasible. Having urban centers lessens the use of cars so people can use public transportation—less congestion, pollution, and use of petroleum products.
(5) This distractor is plausible if the test taker misinterpreted the information about the need for groundwater and believed citizens needed to conserve. Based on the information, having urban centers helps conserve the use of water, so there is no need to limit water use.

34.
(1) This distractor is plausible if the test taker read only the part of the excerpt that said, "Violence often brings about momentary results." Based on the information, violence is destructive and brings about momentary results, but nonviolence is long term; the remainder of the information tells about the positive results using nonviolent actions.
(2) This distractor is plausible if the test taker read only the words "willingness to suffer and sacrifice" at the bottom of the excerpt. There is no evidence in the information that suggests giving up without protest. Dr. King felt people should be willing to sacrifice for the good of the cause.
(3) This is the correct answer. The information states that during nonviolent resistance no person commits an illegal act or violence while working towards equal rights.
(4) This distractor is plausible if the test taker read only the first line that says to accept passively an unjust system. There is no evidence in the information that suggests anyone should accept inequality. The main idea of the information is to encourage those oppressed to use nonviolent methods to gain equality.
(5) This distractor is plausible if the test taker read only the portion of paragraph three that says obey unjust laws. The first paragraph of the information suggests that cooperating with unjust laws is to passively accept it. Nonviolent means are a way to send a message that a law is unjust.

35.
(1) This distractor is plausible if the test taker believed that Dr. King's ideas were meant only for African Americans. Although the information centered mostly on the injustice of the African American population, there were those of other ethnicities that stood beside them in protest.

(2) This distractor is plausible if the test taker believed that the message in this excerpt was to break laws. There is no information that suggests breaking all laws. The oppressed are generally fighting for equality because of prejudice and segregation. All laws do not pertain to these specific issues.

(3) This distractor is plausible if the test taker believed that expressing opinions was not the same as free speech in a controlled assembly of protesters. The entire reading is based on expressing opinions through nonviolent actions.

(4) This distractor is plausible if the test taker believed the only way to fight is to use violence. There is no mention in the excerpt about using guns. The entire reading is based on expressing opinions through nonviolent actions.

(5) This is the correct answer. The information is about people working freely together to fight an unjust system. The First Amendment protects the right to assemble.

36.
(1) This is the correct answer. Dr. King believed that if each individual would fight injustices in nonviolent ways, then each person was impacting change.

(2) This distractor is plausible if the test taker believed this was the way to obtain justice. This saying involves violence in its message; whatever someone does to an individual gives them the right to do the same to the other individual.

(3) This distractor is plausible if the test taker has the opinion that this is true. There is no law that says people should die if they don't fight for a cause. Military actions have their own code of justice.

(4) This distractor is plausible if the test taker interpreted the message as getting what you want by any methods. This sentence suggests that any means possible is a means to an individual's goal. This does not take into account anyone else's goals. It also suggests that violent methods could be used. This was not Dr. King's message.

(5) This distractor is plausible if the test taker shares this opinion. This opinion can be interpreted as meaning that all decisions a government makes, even if poor ones, will be supported by the individual. A test taker might project this attitude onto Dr. King if the test taker believed that even through the bad times, Dr. King still went on with his mission. This expression does not fully express the values of everyone, especially of oppressed or marginalized groups. It suggests complacency about injustices that occur. Dr. King's message does not support this attitude. He felt people should protest injustices and try to get them changed.

37.
(1) This distractor is plausible if the test taker misinterpreted the maps. Although the British and Dutch had control of the Guianas in 1790, they still had control over this region, and none others, in 1828.

(2) This distractor is plausible if the test taker did not know when WWI took place. World War I (1914–1918) had not occurred before either of these dates.

(3) This is the correct answer. As the key in the 1828 map indicates, the blue areas are nations that became independent, and the 1790 map shows from which countries they gained their freedom.

(4) This distractor is plausible if the test taker misinterpreted the maps. The maps clearly indicate that they are showing possessions and how these changed hands. There is no indication of immigration on these maps.

(5) This distractor is plausible if the test taker reversed the years of the maps. As the key in the 1828 map indicates, the blue areas show nations that became independent, and the 1790 map shows from which countries they gained their freedom. Spain lost its control.

38.
(1) This is the correct answer. The Acts affected daily business because stamps were required on all legal documents, permits, commercial contracts, newspapers, wills, pamphlets, and playing cards in the American colonies. The stamp was proof that the stamp tax was paid. The Act was enacted in order to defray the cost of maintaining the military presence protecting the colonies. This act and others like it forced businesses and consumers to pay more for products, and it was another form of taxation without representation.

(2) This distractor is plausible if the test taker believed that since this speech was by Patrick Henry, he probably gave speeches all over the colonies. The information concerns Patrick Henry's speech to the Second Virginia Convention in 1775. The battles began in 1775. There is no indication that he spoke in other colonies.

(3) This distractor is plausible if the test taker felt that most people were unaffected by the British oppression and upcoming war. Based on the time line, people's lives were far from peaceful and quiet. They were being prepared for war and objected to British rule.

(4) This distractor is plausible if the test taker misinterpreted the time line and thought the war was ending when it was just beginning. The last two lines of the speech specifically say the war was inevitable and would come.

(5) This distractor is plausible if the test taker believed that the dates on the time line, indicating the battles at Lexington, Concord, and Trenton, were enough proof that the colonists won the war. The battles only span a short time on the time line, and the war did not end until the Battle of Yorktown in 1781. The test taker, knowing the colonists did win the war, incorrectly guessed this answer.

39.
(1) This distractor is plausible if the test taker did not know the dates of the attack on Pearl Harbor. Pearl Harbor occurred in 1941. This brought the United States into WWII.

(2) This distractor is plausible if the test taker did not know the dates of the Civil War. The U.S. Civil War took place between the Northern and Southern states of the United States. The war began in 1861.

(3) This distractor is plausible if the test taker believes that there has always been slavery. The struggle between the North and South refers to the U.S. Civil War, and the struggle of the slaves to escape to the North occurred at this time.

(4) This distractor is plausible if the test taker did not know the dates of the Industrial Revolution, or the test taker may have instead been thinking about the American Revolution. The Industrial Revolution began in the United States in 1865, and the American Revolution began in 1775.

(5) This is the correct answer. Although not specifically stated, the dates and names provided evidence of the American Revolution. Fighting for freedom was another clue.

40.
- (1) This distractor is plausible if the test taker believed that a war would be better fought and won if there were good roads on which to travel. Based on the excerpt, the entire speech is about freedom and liberty. There is no mention of needing roads and highways.
- **(2) This is the correct answer. Patrick Henry states that "we shall not fight our battles alone . . . there is a just God who presides over the destinies of nations." The entire speech is about freedom and liberty.**
- (3) This distractor is plausible if the test taker only recalled that 3 million people were going to fight. The test taker might have assumed there were weapons. The entire speech is about freedom and liberty. The specific type of armament is not mentioned—only people, liberty, and God are mentioned.
- (4) This distractor is plausible if the test taker read only the facts on the time line. The entire speech is about freedom and liberty. Although tea and sugar are mentioned in the time line, they are not mentioned as a way to victory.
- (5) This distractor is plausible if the test taker only recalled that 3 million people were going to fight. The test taker might have assumed they were a trained army. The entire speech is about freedom and liberty. There is no mention of the methods used to train the army.

41.
- (1) This distractor is plausible if the test taker thought about other fights for liberty and freedom, such as Dr. King, and assumed this one was similar. A non-violent protest would not have helped in terms of the American Revolution. Although there was protesting (some of it violent), most of the ones who needed to hear the demands of the colonists were in Britain.
- (2) This distractor is plausible if the test taker regarded both Patrick Henry and a clergyman as fighting for a cause. A clergyman, however, would not need a war to help the homeless, but Patrick Henry believed that war to free the colonies was inevitable, and he welcomed a war.
- (3) This distractor is plausible if the test taker believed that the British were fighting for the same cause as the colonists. In the colonies and in Britain, there were British people loyal to King George III, and they did would not want to go to war as a first choice. These people would have been happy to continue making demands of the colonists. They did not fight for their own liberty; instead, they fought to keep the colonists from having freedom.
- **(4) This is the correct answer. The speech talks about using a method of war to bring about freedom and liberty. An abolitionist who wants to end slavery would want a war and, in fact, would get a war—the U.S. Civil War.**
- (5) This distractor is plausible if the test taker believed that those who did not support the cause of Patrick Henry and the colonists should leave. Someone leaving the country to avoid a war is contrary to what Patrick Henry was expressing—to fight for liberty.

42.
- (1) This distractor is plausible if the test taker was confused about which nations comprised the Allied forces. Germany was not part of the Allied effort and tried to sink Ally supply ships.
- (2) This distractor is plausible if the test taker did not realize that Australia was in the Indian Ocean. Although part of Britain at the time, Australia was too far from enemy ships.
- (3) This distractor is plausible if the test taker knew that Brazil was along the Atlantic coast. Brazil was not part of the Allied forces and was too far from enemy ships.
- (4) This distractor is plausible if the test taker knew that Japan took part in WWII, but did not understand the role of Japan in this war. Japan was an enemy of the Allies, especially after Peal Harbor. In addition, Japan is in the Pacific Ocean.
- **(5) This is the correct answer. Great Britain was part of the Allied forces that were being attacked by Germany.**

43.
- (1) This distractor is plausible if the test taker interpreted Fact B to mean the Ghanaian Empire fell when the Muslims came. The facts mention trade between the two areas; this indicates that Ghana was an equal participant.
- (2) This distractor is plausible if the test taker believed the increase in trade brought the Europeans who colonized Africa at this time. There is no mention of European colonies in Facts A and B, although Europeans did colonize Africa much later.
- **(3) This is the correct answer. As stated in Fact A, Ghana is in West Africa and traded with Muslim traders of North Africa. Fact B states that many Ghanaian people became Muslim. It was through trading that the influence of the Muslims resulted.**
- (4) This distractor is plausible if the test taker read about gold in Fact A and then assumed there was a decrease in its value because of all the trading. Fact A mentions that gold from West Africa was traded with the Arab traders of North Africa. This indicates that it was a valuable commodity.
- (5) This distractor is plausible if the test taker is unfamiliar with the geography of Africa and believed that a road could be built across this desert. It is difficult to travel through the Saharan Desert. Although it has been done, the facts do not mention this area.

44.
- (1) This distractor is plausible if the test taker saw the flags covered only a small portion of the world. By having flags in even a few regions of the world shows that Uncle Sam was very engaged in world affairs.
- (2) This distractor is plausible if the test taker believed the flag in Uncle Sam's hand might be placed in Russia. Alaska was purchased from Russia. It was called Seward's Folly because many people thought he was crazy to buy land so far north.
- (3) This distractor is plausible if the test taker saw the flag in the Hawaii but thought that he didn't have all the islands. Although the Hawaiian people may not have liked the United States for their incursion into their land, Uncle Sam was delighted, as shown in the cartoon.
- **(4) This is the correct answer. Based on the cartoon, Uncle Sam is placing U.S. flags in regions all over the world. These places are areas acquired through the Spanish-American War. Uncle Sam sees value in having these acquired areas.**
- (5) This distractor is plausible if the test taker believed that everyone celebrated the 4th of July as Independence

Day. In the cartoon, Uncle Sam is not concerned with celebrating July 4th; he is more interested in the countries he has acquired that no longer have independence.

45.
- **(1) This is the correct answer. Based on the information, farmers and other people that live in rural areas are moving to large urban areas, such as Mexico City, for jobs.**
- (2) This distractor is plausible if the test taker believed that a retired person moving to Poland would need city advantages. Based on the information, people in developing countries were moving from rural areas into the urban areas. A retiring Polish family returning to a rural area in Poland would not need the advantages of living in a city.
- (3) This distractor is plausible if the test taker did not equate farming with rural areas. If the test taker knew that Tel Aviv is a large city in Israel, then moving outside Tel Aviv might not seem rural. However, this answer is opposite of the information. This family is moving to a rural area where farming typically takes place.
- (4) This distractor is plausible if the test taker believed that moving to a town was similar to moving to a rural area. Although there is no mention about whether the Turkish welder lives in a rural area, most likely, with a skill such as his, he lives in a city where there would be more need for welding services. The information states that he is moving to a town in Germany. Germany is a developed country with many large cities and towns where a welder could find work.
- (5) This distractor is plausible if the test taker believed that moving to a less crowded island meant it was less rural. The option did not state that the island was rural or that the farmer would continue to farm. This is a scenario whereby a rural citizen in Java is urged to move to a more rural island.

46.
- (1) This distractor is plausible if the test taker believes that the more people who move to the cities created greater competition for jobs. There may be a shortage of jobs, but if more workers are moving to the city to get jobs, there will be plenty of workers.
- (2) This distractor is plausible if the test taker believes that too many people will mean not enough businesses or industries to absorb all the workers. However, industries will need workers, and with the workers, industry will likely expand.
- (3) This distractor is plausible if the test taker believes that too few jobs will mean less to trade. With more workers and expanded industries, trade should increase.
- **(4) This is the correct answer. The information clearly states in the last paragraph that there are often housing shortages because of the influx of families into the cities.**
- (5) This distractor is plausible if the test taker misinterprets a shortage of solid waste to mean a lack of industries creating waste. There is likely to be more waste with more people living in one place.

47.
- (1) This distractor is plausible if the test taker interprets the word *dependence* as a negative outcome for developing countries that want to be independent. However, developing countries need more international trade to raise the standard of living.
- (2) This distractor is plausible if the test taker believes that having a dependency on agricultural products means there will be less economic development. However, there will still be a need for agricultural products to feed the people in the growing cities. Agriculture typically happens in the rural areas adjacent to the cities.
- (3) This distractor is plausible if the test taker reads in the passage that many problems go along with people moving to cities. However, there is no way to know if the total population will decrease or increase; the information only tells that there will be a shift in where the population lives.
- (4) This distractor is plausible if the test taker is confused about the make-up and boundaries of urban versus rural areas. However, there will be more need for health care in the urban areas as more people move there.
- **(5) This is the correct answer. Because much of the rural population is moving to the large urban cities, the percentage of people in the rural areas will decrease.**

48.
- **(1) This is the correct answer. By organizing a voter registration drive, students are doing something for the country and not expecting anything in return. It is a selfless act. They hope people will do their civic duty by voting.**
- (2) This distractor is plausible if the test taker believed that asking Congress to increase social security benefits would help others in the country. The senior citizens are asking for help from Congress, not giving to a greater cause that would help the country.
- (3) This distractor is plausible if the test taker believed that Congress was helping others in the country by building new highways. The congressmen are asking for funds to help their own regions, not giving to a greater cause that would help the country.
- (4) This distractor is plausible if the test taker believed the students were helping all people in the country. Although these students are protesting in Washington, D.C., it is for something that will help only college students, not all citizens.
- (5) This distractor is plausible if the test taker believed that going to the nation's capital helped all people. These students are raising funds for a school trip. They are only helping themselves.

49.
- (1) This distractor is plausible if the test taker was confused about the Northern and Southern Hemispheres or did not know what countries comprised Europe. Based on the key of the map, there was little development of trading south of the equator as compared to the north (8 south of the equator; 27 north of the equator).
- **(2) This is the correct answer. Because of the travels of Dias and de Gama, trading routes were established and European countries set up trading posts in Africa and Asia as shown on the map.**
- (3) This distractor is plausible if the test taker was unable to understand the impact of the travels of these two explorers or misinterpreted the map key. The explorations of Dias and de Gama impacted the trading centers. Their travels are shown along the west coast of Africa, part of the east coast of Africa, and over to India.

(4) This distractor is plausible if the test taker misinterpreted the map or made an assumption that if trade routes were in the Eastern Hemisphere, they happened in the Western Hemisphere during the same period. Although this is true, the map does not show North and South America.
(5) This distractor is plausible if the test taker believed that trading ships did go to Australia, but did not have permanent ports. There are trading posts just north of Australia and test takers might have thought they were part of Australia. Based on the map, there were no trading ports in Australia at this time.

50.
(1) This distractor is plausible if the test taker misinterpreted the map key. Based on the map key, there was no wagon construction, only grants to railroads.
(2) This is the correct answer. Based on the key to the map, the yellow areas show grants to railroads, the pink shows grants to states for construction, the dark pink shows grants for wagon roads, and the dark blue shows an overlap area for both. These grants were provided by the federal government as suggested by the title of the map.
(3) This distractor is plausible if the test taker did not read the title of the map. The title of the map states that there were states that received government grants, and the key shows which states received railroad grants.
(4) This distractor is plausible if the test taker misinterpreted the map key. Almost no railroads or wagon roads were constructed in Indian Territory.
(5) This distractor is plausible if the test taker believed that grants were awarded only between 1828 and 1871. The map shows grants between 1828 and 1871. Grants before this time cannot be determined from this map.

Science

*Exclusively provided and written by the GED Testing Service, answer explanations (rationales) for each test question are provided here for the Full-Length Official GED Practice Test.

1.
   (1) The test takers who are not very familiar with seeing the information in graphic format might select this alternative. The candidate needs to carefully read the graph and compare the average rainfall for each city for the month specified. During the month of February, the average rainfall for city 1 is 6.0 inches and for city 2 is 2.75 inches. These are not very similar numbers.
   (2) The test takers who are not very familiar with seeing the information in graphic format might select this alternative. During the month of September, the average rainfall for city 1 is 2.0 inches and for city 2 is 3.4 inches. The rainfall for these two cities is not very similar for the month of September.
   (3) The test takers who are not very familiar with seeing the information in graphic format might select this alternative. However, during the month of May, the average rainfall for city 1 is 6 inches and for city 2 is 2.75 inches. These are very different numbers.
   (4) This is the correct answer. The average rainfall during the month of March for city 1 is 3.6 inches and for city 2 is 3.4 inches. These readings are very similar.
   (5) The test takers who are not very familiar with seeing the information in graphic format might select this alternative. However, during the month of November, the average rainfall for city 1 is 5.4 inches and for city 2 is 3.1 inches. These are very different numbers.

2.
Candidates need to interpret the information given in a tabular format and apply that information to the second table. An object will sink in water if its density (mass/volume) is greater than that of the water. The density of water at normal temperature is 1 (1 gram/cubic centimeter). Since all the sample cubes have the same volume (let's say one cubic centimeter), it is the mass of the material that is the deciding factor for whether the material will sink or float.
   (1) From the first table, it is clear that the only sample materials that floated have a mass less than 1.00 g. The test takers who fail to interpret the information in the first table might select this alternative. Sample material A will not float in water since its mass is greater than 1.00 g.
   (2) This is the correct answer. Sample material B is the only one that has mass less than 1.00 g.
   (3) The test takers who fail to interpret the information in the first table might select this alternative. Sample material C will not float in water since its mass is greater than 1.00 g.
   (4) The test takers who fail to interpret the information in the first table might select this alternative. Sample material D will not float in water since its mass is greater than 1.00 g.
   (5) The test takers who fail to interpret the information in the first table might select this alternative. Sample material E will not float in water since its mass is greater than 1.00 g.

3.
   (1) The test takers might select this alternative because the speed of sound is much higher in solids than in air. Therefore, they could hear the arrival of rescuers faster by being closer to the floor. However, inhaling toxic fumes is the primary cause of fatality during a fire, and hearing the arrival of the rescuers will not be helpful to survival.
   (2) The test takers might select this alternative since the words "flame-retardant materials" might sound attractive to them. However, inhaling toxic fumes is the primary cause of fatality during a fire.
   (3) The test takers might select this alternative because getting close to the floor will allow a person to test the temperature of the fire more easily. However, inhaling toxic fumes is the primary cause of fatality during a fire.
   (4) The test takers might select this alternative because extinguishing the fire with the least amount of effort would sound attractive. However, inhaling toxic fumes is the primary cause of fatality during a fire.
   (5) This is the correct answer. Fire produces smoke and hot harmful gases that are lighter than the air. Air is cleaner and cooler near the floor. It is best for a person to be closer to the floor while waiting for rescuers to come.

4.
   (1) The test takers need to understand the information given in the tabular format and identify which elements are most abundant in Earth's crust. If the test takers are not interpreting the information in the table correctly, they might select this alternative.
   (2) The test takers might select this alternative because the first two elements are the most abundant in Earth's crust. However, the third element in the alternative is from the seawater, not from Earth's crust.
   (3) This is the correct answer. Based on the information given in the table, oxygen, silicon, and aluminum are the most abundant elements in Earth's crust.
   (4) The test takers might select this alternative because sodium, magnesium, and calcium are most abundant in seawater. However, the question specifically asks about the most abundant element in Earth's crust.
   (5) The test takers might select this alternative because these are the most abundant elements both in seawater and Earth's crust. However, the question asks about the most abundant element in Earth's crust.

5.
   (1) The test takers might select this alternative since both snake and grass are mentioned in the stimulus. Those who not familiar with food web diagrams may misread the arrows in the food web and might select this alternative. Based on the food web shown, snakes are secondary consumers and feed on primary consumers, not producers.
   (2) This is the correct answer. Based on the information given in the food web, the hawk eats shrews, snakes, birds, and squirrels.
   (3) The test takers might select this alternative because squirrels are the first primary consumers listed in the

food web. The test takers who are not very familiar with food web diagrams could assume that since rabbits are listed after squirrels in this category, rabbits are consumed by squirrels. However, the squirrels eat grasses and grains.
- (4) The test takers might select this alternative because they could assume that the tertiary consumers could eat organisms from any other level. However, based on the food web shown, the hawk does not eat insects.
- (5) The test takers might select this alternative because those who are not very familiar with food web diagrams could assume that a food web starts with primary consumers. However, the food web begins with producers that include grasses, grains, vegetables, and shrubs.

6.
- (1) The test takers might select this alternative if they fail to interpret the information given in a visual format. However, based on the graph, from A to B, the velocity changes from 20 meters/second to 50 meters/second, and therefore, the object is accelerating.
- **(2) This is the correct answer. Based on the graph, from B to C, the line is flat indicating a constant velocity (no change). This means that the object's acceleration is zero, and therefore, the object is not accelerating.**
- (3) The test takers might select this alternative if they fail to interpret the information given in a visual format. However, based on the graph, from C to D, the velocity changes from 50 meters/second to 90 meters/second, and therefore, the object has experienced acceleration.
- (4) The test takers might select this alternative if they fail to interpret the information given in a visual format. However, based on the graph, from D to E, the velocity changes 90 meters/second to 100 meters/second, and therefore, the object is accelerating.
- (5) The test takers might select this alternative because sometimes the terms *speed* and *acceleration* are used interchangeably. However, the definition of acceleration is a change in velocity. The test takers need to determine if there has been a change in velocity (both speed and direction) from E to A. The object is moving downward with speed changing from 100 meters/second to 20 meters/second. This means that the object has experienced acceleration, even though the speed has decreased.

7.
- (1) The test takers might select this alternative because the stimulus mentions close ecological association between two species involving frequent or permanent cellular contact. However, the relationship between the flea and dog is not at the cellular level.
- (2) The test takers might select this alternative because the stimulus mentions the close association between two species in commensalisms. However, in commensalism, one species benefits while the other is not helped or harmed from the association. In the case of flea and dog, only the flea benefits from this association.
- (3) Some test takers might select this alternative because the flea does not have an association with its host at cellular level. However, the relationship is beneficial to the flea and harmful to the dog.
- (4) The test takers might select this alternative because the stimulus mentions the close association between two species in mutualism. However, in mutualism, both species benefit from the association. In the case of flea and dog, only the flea benefits.
- **(5) This is the correct answer. The dog is harmed from this association while the flea sustains life by absorbing blood from the dog.**

8.
- (1) The test takers might select this alternative if they are not familiar with the different stages of cell division. They might identify the third stage in the process as the daughter cells. However, the daughter cells clearly show the same number of chromosomes as the parent cell in the last stage.
- (2) The test takers might select this alternative because the diagram shows a single cell undergoing changes that might appear as if the cell is going through cell repair. However, the diagram depicts the different stages of cell division.
- (3) The test takers might select this alternative because in the diagram, the cell duplicates the chromosomes at certain stage of the division. At this stage, the chromosome number appears to be more than four. However, by the end of the cell division, each daughter cell has the same number of chromosomes as the parent cell.
- (4) The test takers might select this alternative if they mistakenly identify the third stage of cell division as the daughter cells and then conclude that the chromosomes fail to double properly. However, the diagram does not indicate that the chromosomes fail to double properly during the cell division.
- **(5) This is the correct answer. During mitosis or normal cell division two identical daughter cells are produced from a single cell by replicating the original chromosomes.**

9.
- (1) The test takers might select this alternative if they do not understand the difference between the energy of position and energy of motion. The baseball before it lands has kinetic energy (energy of motion).
- (2) The test takers might select this alternative if they do not understand the difference between the energy of position and energy of motion. An oncoming car (moving car) has kinetic energy.
- (3) The test takers might select this alternative if they assume that the process of turning off the lamp is energy of position. However, turning off an electric lamp is shutting off electrical energy (which is a form of kinetic energy) going through the lamp, not conversion of potential energy to kinetic energy.
- **(4) This is the correct answer. An apple on the tree has potential energy (energy of position), and by falling from the tree, the potential energy is converted to kinetic energy.**
- (5) The test takers might select this alternative if they do not understand the difference between the energy of position and energy of motion. A jogger running the race has kinetic energy.

10.
- (1) The test takers might select this alternative if they assume that the heating period only includes when the temperature is rising. Based on the graph, temperature increases until it reaches 90°C and remains at 90°C for the rest of the heating period.

(2) The test takers might select this alternative if they think that the liquid changed to another compound once the temperature stabilized. However, not enough information is provided to indicate that the liquid was converted to another compound during the heating period. The graph illustrates the boiling of a liquid.

(3) This is the correct answer. From the graph, it appears that during the heating process the temperature of the liquid stays at 90°C over a period of time indicating that the liquid is boiling.

(4) Since the temperature of the liquid at the beginning of the process was –20°C, it is not possible for the liquid to freeze at 90°C during the heating time. The test takers might select this alternative if they are unable to interpret/read the graph.

(5) The test takers might select this alternative if they fail to understand that the boiling of a liquid is illustrated in the graph. Since the temperature stayed at 90°C over a period of time, it is not possible that the liquid has evaporated completely as soon as it reached 90°C.

11.
(1) The test takers might select this alternative if they are unable to interpret/read the food pyramid. Based on the food pyramid diagram given, in order to maintain a healthy dietary intake, a person needs 2–3 servings of diary products and 3–5 servings of the vegetable group.

(2) The test takers might select this alternative if they are unable to interpret/read the food pyramid. The bread group comprises the largest section (6–11 servings) of the food pyramid, not the meat products (2–3 servings).

(3) The test takers might select this alternative if they are unable to interpret/read the food pyramid. Based on the food pyramid diagram, fats and sweets should be used sparingly.

(4) This is the correct answer. In order to maintain a healthy dietary intake, a person should be having more servings of vegetables (3–5 servings), fresh fruits (2–4 servings), and grain cereals (6–11 servings) than servings of meat (2–3 servings) and fat (use sparingly).

(5) The test takers might select this alternative if they are unable to interpret/read the food pyramid. The recommendation based on the food pyramid is to have larger portion of grains in order to maintain a healthy dietary intake.

12.
(1) The test takers might select this alternative if they are unable to interpret the growth pattern from the graph. Based on the graph, girls grow faster than boys only at age 13.

(2) The test takers might select this alternative if they are unable to interpret growth pattern from the graph. Based on the graph, there is no difference in growth rate at ages 0–9. However, at and after the age of 13 years, there are differences in the growth pattern of these two groups.

(3) The test takers might select this alternative if they are unable to interpret the growth pattern from the graph. Based on the graph, girls exhibit the highest growth rate at ages 9–13.

(4) The test takers might select this alternative if they are unable to interpret the growth pattern from the graph. Based on the graph, the only age interval during which the boys grow faster than girls is between the ages 13–18.

(5) This is the correct answer. Based on the graph, boys grow at a faster rate than girls at ages 13–18.

13.
(1) The test takers might select this alternative if they are unable to interpret the information given. When a layer of water builds between the rubber tires of the vehicle and the road surface, hydroplaning occurs. It is unlikely for hydroplaning to occur on a dry concrete road.

(2) This is the correct answer. Hydroplaning occurs when a tire encounters more water than it can dissipate. The tire then skates on a sheet of water with little, if any, direct road contact, resulting in loss of control.

(3) The test takers might select this alternative if they are unable to interpret the information given. Hydroplaning is not a sport. It is a road hazard during wet or icy driving conditions.

(4) The test takers might select this alternative if they are unable to interpret the information given. It is unlikely for hydroplaning to occur in hot dry weather. Water is required for this process to happen.

(5) The test takers might select this alternative if they are unable to interpret the information given. Dirt roads may provide more friction, which will produce a greater resistance to slipping.

14.
(1) The test takers might select this alternative if they are unable to interpret the pattern of inheritance for cystic fibrosis illustrated in the pedigree diagram. Based on the information and diagram, persons showing the cystic fibrosis disease is present only in the second generation.

(2) The test takers might select this alternative if they are unable to interpret the pattern of inheritance for cystic fibrosis illustrated in the pedigree diagram. Based on the information and diagram, both male and female show cystic fibrosis.

(3) The test takers might select this alternative if they are unable to interpret the pattern of inheritance for cystic fibrosis illustrated in the pedigree diagram. Based on the information and diagram, the third generation shows children with no disease even though the father suffered from the disease.

(4) This is the correct answer. The fact that there is a third generation with a father who suffered the disease shows that an individual with cystic fibrosis can live long enough to have children.

(5) The test takers might select this alternative if they are unable to interpret the pattern of inheritance for cystic fibrosis illustrated in the pedigree diagram. How the disease affects one gender more than the other is not clear from the information and diagram.

15.
(1) The test takers might select this alternative because "evaporation" is mentioned in the diagram. However, in the water cycle, evaporation is the primary pathway as water moves from the liquid state back into the water cycle as atmospheric water vapor.

(2) This is the correct answer. Condensation is the opposite of evaporation. It occurs when saturated air is cooled below the dew point. Condensation is crucial to the water cycle because it is responsible for the formation of clouds.

(3) The test takers might select this alternative if they fail to interpret the process illustrated in the diagram. Elevation is the height above a fixed reference point.
(4) The test takers might select this alternative if they fail to interpret the process illustrated in the diagram. When cloud particles become too heavy to remain suspended in the air, they fall to Earth as precipitation in the form of rain, snow, sleet, or hail.
(5) The test takers might select this alternative because "runoff" is mentioned in the diagram. When rain or snow falls onto Earth, it starts moving according to the laws of gravity. Surface runoff is water flowing downhill from precipitation.

16.
(1) The test takers might select this alternative if they assume that damaging one part of the brain might impair the ability to detect odors. The corpus callosum connects the left and right cerebral hemispheres. It does not control a person's ability to detect odors.
(2) The test takers might select this alternative if they are unable to understand the information given. The cerebrum controls muscle movements and speech, and interprets messages from the sense organs. Damage to the cerebrum does not affect sleep patterns.
(3) **This is the correct answer. Damage to the hippocampus will affect the ability to form new memories.**
(4) The test takers might select this alternative if they are unable to understand the information given. The cerebellum coordinates motor movement. Damage to the cerebellum could result in uncoordinated, slow movement.
(5) The test takers might select this alternative if they are unable to understand the information given. The left half of the brain controls speech, sensation and movement of the right side of the body, and vision in the right half of the visual field.

17.
(1) The test takers might select this alternative if they do not know which foods contain cholesterol. Proteins from food are the building materials for the body to use in growth and repair. Proteins do not contain cholesterol.
(2) The test takers might select this alternative if they do not know which foods contain cholesterol. Carbohydrates are energy rich foods that do not contain cholesterol.
(3) **This is the correct answer. Cholesterol is found in animal fats. Plants and plant products have only trace amounts of cholesterol.**
(4) The test takers might select this alternative if they do not know which foods contain cholesterol. Vitamins serve as coenzymes that activate enzymes and help them function in the proper way. They do not contain cholesterol.
(5) The test takers might select this alternative if they are unable to understand the information given. Enzymes are catalysts and most enzymes are proteins. They do not contain any cholesterol.

18.
(1) **This is the correct answer. DNA molecules carry the genetic instructions for the development and functioning of all living organisms.**
(2) The test takers might select this alternative if they are unable to understand the information given. DNA molecules encode the instructions for the functioning of the cells.
(3) The test takers might select this alternative if they are unable to understand the information given. Cells use information encoded in the DNA to build different proteins, each with a unique function. This process is the same in all organisms. The amino acid sequence in different organisms shows a lot of similarity, so the chemical similarity of organisms is not due to chance.
(4) The test takers might select this alternative if they are unable to understand the information given. With the current scientific knowledge regarding how genetic information is encoded in organisms, there is no reason to believe that new organisms could be discovered without DNA.
(5) The process in which cell proteins (amino acid sequences in protein) that carry out cell functions are developed is similar in all organisms.

19.
(1) **This is the correct answer. Jupiter has the greatest gravitational force, and it is approximately 2.5 times greater than that of Earth.**
(2) The test takers might select this alternative if they are unable to interpret the relative gravitational forces from the graph. Saturn's gravitational force is similar to that of Earth's. Saturn does not have the greatest gravitational force.
(3) The test takers might select this alternative if they are unable to understand how weight can change based on the gravitational force. Since Pluto's gravitational force is less than that of Earth's, an object weighing one pound on Earth will weigh less on Pluto.
(4) The test takers might select this alternative if they are unable to interpret the relative gravitational forces from the graph. Neptune has greater gravitational force (approximately 1.1) than Mars (approximately 0.4)
(5) The test takers might select this alternative if they are unable to understand how weight can change due to gravitational force changes. An astronaut would weigh more on Neptune than on Earth since Neptune exerts more gravitational pull than Earth.

20.
(1) The test takers might select this alternative because they might consider 2-inch growth as not significant. However, quantitative data in precise units is a critical component of a scientific experiment.
(2) The test takers who are not familiar with the steps involved in scientific methods might select this alternative. However, this is an assumption that is not supported by the data provided.
(3) The test takers who are not familiar with the steps involved in scientific methods might select this alternative thinking that the eleven-year-olds who participated in the study should not have been allowed to eat food in addition to the food supplement. However, the independent variable in this experiment is only the food supplement.
(4) **This is the correct answer. This experiment is lacking a control group. Without the control group, the researcher cannot draw conclusions about the experiment.**
(5) The test takers who are not familiar with the steps involved in scientific methods might select this alternative

thinking that other factors should have been measured during this experiment. However, the dependent variable in this experiment is the rate of growth.

21.
   (1) **This is the correct answer. The leaf shape (waxy surface and drip-tip) is a plant adaptation that helps the plant to survive the heavy rainfall in the rain forest.**
   (2) Broad smooth leaves (waxy surfaces) with narrow to sharp points at the end (drip-tips) do not discourage or prevent animals from climbing on the tree branches. The test takers might select this alternative if they think that the narrow to sharp points at the end of a leaf (drip-tips and waxy surfaces) could be an adaptation that would prevent the animals from climbing on the branches.
   (3) The test takers might select this alternative because the rainforest forest floor does not receive much sunlight. However, the plant adaptation of the leaf shape does not protect the forest floor. Instead, the shape of the leaf helps to shed the excess water that might otherwise accumulate on the leaves and encourage the growth of bacteria and fungi in the warm tropical forest.
   (4) The test takers might select this alternative because leaves provide a place of protection for insects. However, the plant adaptation of the leaf shape is not to provide a place of protection for insects but to shed the excess water that might have otherwise accumulated on the leaves and encouraged the growth of bacteria and fungi in the warm tropical forest.
   (5) The leaf shape (drip-tips) allows the water to drip off the leaves. The test takers might choose this alternative if they do not understand how this plant adaptation is essential for the survival of the plants in an environment with exceptionally high rainfall.

22.
   (1) The test takers might select this alternative if they think that docking the boat along the shore would help avoid the destructive waves of the tsunami. However, the waves rise in height when the tsunami encounters shallow water.
   (2) The test takers might select this alternative if they think that seeking cover on a beach after abandoning the boat would help to avoid the destructive waves. However, the waves rise in height when they encounter shallow water.
   (3) **This is the correct answer. A tsunami has much smaller wave height (amplitude) and very long wavelength in the open ocean compared to near shore.**
   (4) The test takers might select this alternative if they think that staying in the boat after beaching it would help to avoid the destructive waves. However, the waves rise in height when they encounter shallow water and smash into land with destructive forces.
   (5) The test takers might select this alternative if they think that moving the boat to a narrow bay near the shore would help to avoid the destructive waves. However, the waves rise in height when they encounter shallow water and smash into land with destructive forces. A narrow bay near the shore may not be a safe place.

23.
   (1) **This is the correct answer. In this scientific experiment, temperature is the only factor that is different or changed in order to test the hypothesis.**
   (2) The test takers who are not familiar with the steps involved in scientific methods might select this alternative thinking that the petri dishes are the variable in this experiment. In all three environments the same type of petri dishes are used.
   (3) The test takers who are not familiar with the steps involved in scientific methods might select this alternative. "Big Boy" seeds are used in all three environments.
   (4) The test takers who are not familiar with the steps involved in scientific methods might select this alternative. Eight seeds are used for all three environments.
   (5) The test takers who are not familiar with the steps involved in scientific methods might select this alternative. The type of moist paper used in all three environments is the same.

24.
   (1) **This is the correct answer. When completing an experiment, scientists evaluate their results, alter the hypothesis based on the new information gathered, and repeat the tests again until they get results that are reproducible.**
   (2) The test takers who are not familiar with the steps involved in scientific methods might find this alternative attractive thinking that findings that support a hypothesis are the only ones required for the experiment. This is a common misconception.
   (3) The test takers might select this alternative because this is a false assumption many have regarding the nature of scientific experiments. However, important discoveries do not happen every time an experiment is carried out.
   (4) The test takers who are not familiar with the steps involved in scientific methods might select this alternative. However, the tests need to be repeated until reproducible results are obtained.
   (5) The test takers who are not familiar with the steps involved in scientific methods might select this alternative without knowing several attempts need to be completed before developing a process or system that helps show relationships among data.

25.
   (1) The four insects shown in the diagram have antennas. However, they differ greatly in size and shape. The test takers who are not familiar with identifying similarities in the morphological characteristics might select this alternative.
   (2) The test takers might assume that since all four insects have moth parts, they can be grouped together using this characteristic. Those who are not familiar with identifying similarities in the morphological characteristics might select this alternative. However, the mouth parts are not similar for these insects as shown in the diagram.
   (3) Only two of the four insects shown in the diagram have wings therefore this characteristic cannot be used when looking for similar characteristics. The test takers who are not familiar with identifying the morphological characteristics might select this alternative.
   (4) The test takers who are not familiar with identifying the morphological characteristics might select this alternative. However, all four insects shown in the diagram do not have stingers.

- (5) **This is the correct answer. All four insects shown in the diagram have three pairs of legs.**

26.
- (1) The test takers might select this alternative if they are unable to understand that the information is given in a tabular format.
- (2) **This is the correct answer. The total percentage of cells (red blood cells and white blood cells) in blood is 45%.**
- (3) The test takers might select this alternative because 43% is given in the table. However, this includes only red blood cells, not white blood cells.
- (4) The test takers might select this alternative if they subtract the percentage of WBC from the percentage of RBC.
- (5) The test takers might select this alternative if they select only the percentage of WBC.

27.
- (1) **This is the correct answer. When light energy is absorbed by an object, it is converted to heat. In the Northern Hemisphere, there is more daylight during summer, which could make it uncomfortable to wear dark clothes during summer.**
- (2) The test takers might select this alternative since in the stimulus it is mentioned that light energy can also be converted to chemical energy. However, in this case the dark-colored clothes absorb the energy and convert it to heat, not chemical energy.
- (3) The test takers might select this alternative since in the stimulus it is mentioned that some light energy is reflected. However, in this case the dark-colored clothes absorb the energy and convert it to heat, not reflect it back.
- (4) The test takers might select this alternative since in the stimulus it is mentioned that light energy can be converted into different forms of energy. However, in this instance the dark-colored clothes absorb the energy and convert it to heat, not electrical energy.
- (5) The test takers might select this alternative if they think the dark cloth is attracting light energy rather than absorbing it. However, in this instance the light energy is converted into heat energy.

28.
- (1) The test takers might select this alternative if they are not very familiar with what a dentist's work entails. As a health care professional, a dentist generally does not need to check the information given in the table. The person most familiar with the information will be a medical lab technician.
- (2) The test takers might select this alternative if they are not very familiar with what an X-ray technician's work entails. As a health care professional, an X-ray technician normally does not need to check the information given in the table and therefore, may not be the person who is most familiar with the information.
- (3) **This is the correct answer. A medical lab technician will be familiar with information given in the table.**
- (4) The test takers might select this alternative if they are not very familiar with what a physical therapist's work entails. As a health care professional, a physical therapist does not normally need to check the information given in the table and therefore, may not be the person who is most familiar with the information. The person most familiar with the information will be a medical lab technician.
- (5) The test takers might select this alternative if they are not very familiar with what an optometrist's work entails. As a health care professional, an optometrist does not normally need to check the information given in the table and therefore, may not be the person who is most familiar with the information. The person most familiar with the information will be a medical lab technician.

29.
- (1) An asteroid is a small celestial body that orbits around Sun. The diagram illustrates the eclipse of Sun which only occurs at new moon when the Moon passes between Earth and Sun. The test takers might select this alternative if they assume the small object is an asteroid.
- (2) Mars is a planet in the solar system. The diagram illustrates the eclipse of Sun which only occurs at new moon when the Moon passes between Earth and Sun. The test takers might select this alternative if they think the small object is Mars.
- (3) **This is the correct answer. The diagram illustrates the eclipse of the Sun which only occurs at new moon when the Moon passes between Earth and Sun. If the Moon's shadow happens to fall upon Earth's surface at that time, some portion of the Sun's disk will be covered or 'eclipsed' by the Moon, which is visible from Earth.**
- (4) Venus is a planet in the solar system. It is also known as Earth's twin planet. The test takers might select this alternative if they think the small object is Venus.
- (5) A space station is not big enough to eclipse the Sun. The test takers might select this alternative if they think the small object could be a space station.

30.
- (1) The test takers might select this alternative if they assume that saliva can hold the coin in place. However, the information given does not suggest that saliva is used for this experiment.
- (2) There is no magnetic attraction between the coin and the hanger. The test takers might select this alternative if they do not understand how centripetal force works.
- (3) The test takers might select this alternative if they do not understand how centripetal force works. The centripetal force or "center seeking" force is an external force that is required to make an object follow a circular path at a constant speed. When the rotational speed is sufficient, centripetal force directed inward toward the center of the circle will keep the coin in place. If the rotational speed is slow, the coin will not stay in place.
- (4) **This is the correct answer. The centripetal force, which means "center seeking" force, is an external force that is required to make an object follow a circular path at a constant speed. When the rotational speed is sufficient, centripetal force directed inward toward the center of the circle will keep the coin in place.**
- (5) The test takers might select this alternative if they do not understand how centripetal force works. The penny does experience the gravitational force acting on it. However, it is the centripetal force directed inward that keeps the penny in place when it reaches sufficient speed.

31.
- (1) The test takers might select this alternative if they did not comprehend the information given. The question asks

what type of future children might show the symptoms of the disease. The parent is a carrier of the disease.
- (2) The test takers might select this alternative if they did not comprehend the information given. The question asks what type of future children might show the symptoms of the disease. The parent is a carrier of the disease. Only male children develop the symptoms.
- **(3) This is the correct answer. Only sons will develop the disease.**
- (4) The test takers might select this alternative if they did not comprehend the information given. The question asks what type of future children might show the symptoms of the disease. The disease affects only male children, not female children.
- (5) The test takers might select this alternative if they did not comprehend the information given. The question asks what type of future children might show the symptoms of the disease. The disease affects only male children. Daughters will not be affected.

32.
- (1) The test takers might select this alternative if they are not careful. Chewing is under conscious control. However, this is not the only stage of digestion that is under conscious control.
- (2) The breakdown of food in the stomach is a complicated process that is not under conscious control. The test takers might select this alternative since breaking down of food is mentioned in the stimulus.
- (3) Chewing is under conscious control. The breakdown of food in the stomach is a complicated process that is not under conscious control. The test takers might select this alternative since both are mentioned in the stimulus.
- (4) All the stages of digestion are not under conscious control. The test takers might select this alternative if they are not familiar with the different stages of digestion.
- **(5) This is the correct answer. Only chewing and swallowing are under conscious control.**

33.
- (1) The test takers might select this alternative if they do not comprehend the information given in the stimulus. This method will address the threat from only the right side, which the fly will be able to avoid.
- (2) The test takers might select this alternative if they do not comprehend the information given in the stimulus. This method will address the threat from only the left side, which the fly will be able to avoid.
- (3) The test takers might select this alternative if they do not comprehend the information given in the stimulus. This method will address the threat from only above, which the fly will be able to avoid.
- (4) The test takers might select this alternative if they do not comprehend the information given in the stimulus. This method will address the threat from only below, which the fly will be able to avoid.
- **(5) This is the correct answer. The fly will not be able to handle threats from more than one direction.**

34.
- (1) The test takers might select this alternative if they incorrectly read the information given in the graph. Based on the graph, as the temperature rises from 600 to 800 Kelvin, the volume increases from 2 to 3.5 liters.
- **(2) This is the correct answer. Based on the graph, as the temperature rises from 600 to 800 Kelvin the volume increases from 1.5 to 2 liters.**
- (3) The test takers might select this alternative if they fail to identify the pattern illustrated in the graph. The graph's pattern shows volume increases as temperature increases.
- (4) The test takers might select this alternative since pressure is mentioned in the stimulus and might incorrectly assume that the graph is showing the pressure temperature relationship. However, the graph is illustrating the volume temperature relationship under constant pressure.
- (5) The test takers might select this alternative if they fail to read the *x*-axis label that clearly indicates Kelvin as a unit of measure for temperature.

35.
- (1) The climate is drier on the leeward side. The prevailing winds lose the moisture content by the time they reach the leeward side. The test takers might select this alternative if they fail to understand the information presented in the visual format.
- (2) Plants that need large amounts of water may not be found on the leeward side since little rain occurs on this side. The test takers might select this alternative if they fail to understand the information presented in the visual format.
- **(3) This is the correct answer. Based on the diagram, on the windward side of the mountain, there is condensation of water vapor carried by the wind. This leads to cloud formation and precipitation.**
- (4) The test takers might select this alternative if they fail to understand the information presented in the visual format. Based on the diagram, on the windward side of the mountain, the warm moist air coming from the prevailing wind condenses forming clouds. This results in precipitation only on the windward side.
- (5) The test takers might select this alternative if they fail to understand the information presented in the visual format. Based on the diagram, the prevailing winds lose the moisture content by the time they reach the leeward side.

36.
- (1) The test takers might select this alternative if they fail to understand the difference between weight and apparent weight. Weight is the measurement of gravitational force acting on an object. Richard's original weight is not a factor that affects the reading on the scale.
- (2) The test takers might select this alternative if they think that there is no difference between the weight and apparent weight. The size of the elevator does not affect the apparent weight on the scale.
- (3) The test takers might select this alternative if they assume the strength of the scale affects the weight. The strength of the scale does not affect the apparent weight of an object.
- **(4) This is the correct answer. For a body supported in a stationary position, the normal force balances Earth's gravitational force, so apparent weight has the same magnitude as actual weight. In an elevator, a spring scale will register an increase in a person's (apparent) weight as the elevator starts to accelerate upward. This is because a scale does not measure an object's actual weight, but rather measures the force that it exerts on the scale.**

(5) The floor level at which the elevator begins does not affect the apparent weight of an object. The test takers might select this alternative if they fail to understand the difference between the weight and apparent weight.

37.
(1) The test taker might select this alternative if they assume that spring water is pure and free of all minerals. Spring water contains dissolved minerals depending on the geology through which the spring has traveled. If used in an iron, spring water will cause build up.
(2) The test taker might select this alternative thinking that tap water is treated to remove pathogens and bacteria to make it safe for human consumption and therefore, free of all impurities. However, the minerals are not removed from drinking water.
(3) **This is the correct answer. Distilled water contains only molecules of water, and virtually all impurities are removed through distillation.**
(4) The test taker might select this alternative if they assume that hard water does not have dissolved minerals in it. However, hard water has high mineral content, usually ions of calcium and magnesium. When boiled, water evaporates leaving behind a deposit of calcium and magnesium.
(5) The test taker might select this alternative if they assume that cold water contains less impurities and is therefore pure. However, minerals present in the water will be left behind in the iron.

38.
(1) **This is the correct answer. Potential and kinetic energies comprise all type of energies.**
(2) The test taker might select this alternative if they are not familiar with different forms of energy. Elastic energy is a form of potential energy, and inelastic energy is a form of kinetic energy.
(3) The test taker might select this alternative if they are not familiar with different forms of energy. Harmonic and unharmonious energy waves are forms of kinetic energy.
(4) The test taker might select this alternative if they are not familiar with different forms of energy. An object in inertia has potential energy and in of non-inertia has kinetic energy.
(5) The test taker might select this alternative if they are not familiar with different forms of energy. Gravitational and negative gravitational energy (or antigravitational energy) are forms of potential energy.

39.
(1) The test takers who fail to interpret the information given in graphic format might select this alternative. However, based on the graph, an increase in temperature raised the solubility of four compounds.
(2) **This is the correct answer. The solubility of most compounds increases. Solubility of one compound decreased as the temperature increased.**
(3) The test takers might select this alternative since four out of the five compounds had increasing solubility with increasing temperature. However, based on the graph, the dissolving rate was very different for the five compounds given.
(4) This conclusion cannot be reached from the given information and graph. The test takers might select this alternative if they generalize that these compounds behave in the same manner in different solvents.

(5) The test takers might select this alternative if they assume that solubility has few applications in everyday life. However, from the information and graph, this conclusion cannot be reached.

40.
(1) **This is the correct answer. Seals are higher up in the food chain than the fish, and the mercury level builds up in seals as they eat fish which have mercury in their bodies.**
(2) The level of mercury in the ocean water is less than the level of mercury in the fish that seals have eaten. Also, seals get their water from their food. The test takers might select this alternative thinking that the major source of mercury in the seals body comes directly from the contaminated water.
(3) The test takers might select this alternative if they assume that the seals feed on the waste materials from the factories. However, they feed on organisms that eat the contaminated waste products.
(4) The test taker might select this alternative if they assume that seals need mercury in their diet. However, mercury is a toxic substance that enters the body of seals through the food chain. Seals do not need mercury in their diet.
(5) The test taker might select this alternative if they assume that seals feed on algae. However, seals eat a variety of fish, crustacean, and mollusks. The stimulus says seals feed on mainly smaller water animals. They do not feed on algae.

41.
(1) **This is the correct answer. The purpose of the pressure cooker in home canning is to sterilize the food to prevent spoilage.**
(2) Using the pressure cooker kills the bacteria. It does not sweeten the food. The test takers might select this alternative if they do not understand the canning process.
(3) The test takers might select this alternative if they do not understand the canning process. Color of the food is not preserved by the pressure cooking.
(4) The test taker might select this alternative if they do not understand the canning process. Using the pressure cooker during the canning process does not increase the vitamin content of the food.
(5) The test takers might select this alternative if they do not understand the canning process. Using the pressure cooker during the canning process does not eliminate the odor of the food.

42.
(1) The test takers who misinterpret the diagram might select this alternative. Since the freshwater fish skeletons are shown in the top section of the rocks, the test takers might assume that a freshwater lake has always covered this area.
(2) The test takers who fail to interpret the diagram correctly might select this alternative. However, the oldest rocks show the fossils of marine clams and snails which indicates that the area is currently not under ocean.
(3) The test takers who misinterpret the diagram might select this alternative. The chronological sequence indicates that the area was under ocean and then on land. The dinosaurs existed in this area after the area was above sea level.

(4) **This is the correct answer. The chronological sequence indicates that the area was under ocean, then on land, and then under a river or lake.**
(5) The section does not indicate that the area was under sea for the entire time. The test takers who misinterpret the diagram might select this alternative.

43.
(1) Praying mantises do not specifically feed on pollinators (bees, butterflies, etc.). The test takers may select this alternative since it is mentioned that in the process of controlling the harmful insects, praying mantises kill some beneficial ones as well. However, the question asks for the characteristic most important in improving the garden environment.
(2) **This is the correct answer. Praying mantises prey upon many harmful insects, such as aphids, and are considered a form of "biological pest control" by gardeners.**
(3) Praying mantises are predatory insects. They do not feed on weeds. The test takers may select this alternative if they are not aware that preying mantises are predatory.
(4) The test takers may select this alternative if they assume that these animals improve the garden environment by transferring beneficial genes to plants. However, they do not transfer genes to garden plants.
(5) The test takers may select this alternative if they assume that these animals improve the garden environment by transferring color pigments to plants. However, they camouflage in with surrounding plant life and do not transfer color pigments to plants.

44.
(1) The test taker might select this alternative since drawing a family pedigree (history) chart is a helpful shorthand method of documenting family relationships. However, family pedigree is not the best scientific method in deciding whether twins are identical.
(2) The test taker might select this alternative if they assume that identical twins have identical cholesterol levels. However, identical blood cholesterol levels do not confirm whether twins are identical.
(3) **This is the correct answer. DNA analysis is used to prove genetic relationships. Identical twins will have identical genetic profiles.**
(4) The test taker might select this alternative because a saliva test is used as a diagnostic tool to uncover biochemical imbalances or steroid hormones in the blood. However, this test data cannot determine whether twins are identical.
(5) The test taker might select this alternative if they assume that information about grandparents might provide data to determine if the twins are identical. However, grandparents' birth dates do not provide data to determine whether twins are identical.

45.
(1) The test taker might select this alternative if they assume the birds exhibited an instinctive behavior by taking cream from milk bottles. However, based on the information, different types of birds did not know how to remove the milk from the bottles instinctively. It was a learned behavior.

(2) **This is the correct answer. Young birds learned the behavior from older birds, and different types of birds imitated the birds that already knew how to puncture the foil caps to remove milk from the bottles.**
(3) The test taker might select this alternative if they did not comprehend the information given in the stimulus. Learned behavior is not inherited from parents. Parents do not pass learned behaviors to the offspring. The offspring must learn the behavior.
(4) The test taker might select this alternative because it states in the stimulus that many birds started taking the milk from the milk bottles not only in England, but also in central Europe. However, the birds' natural diet does not include milk.
(5) The test taker might select this alternative if they assume this specific bird displayed highly advanced behavior. However, birds tend to show similar behavior to accomplish certain goals. They learn this by observation and imitation. The birds learned the behavior from other birds.

46.
(1) The test taker might select this alternative if they did not comprehend the information given in the diagram. The flight from Chicago to San Francisco is outside the jet stream and will not benefit from the jet stream.
(2) The test taker might select this alternative if they did not comprehend the information given in the diagram. The flight from San Francisco to Houston is totally outside the jet stream, and the flight will not benefit from the jet stream.
(3) **This is the correct answer. The jet stream will help this flight to reduce flight time.**
(4) The test taker might select this alternative if they did not comprehend the information given in the diagram. The flight path is outside the jet stream from Boston to Houston.
(5) The test taker might select this alternative if they did not comprehend the information given in the diagram. The flight path is outside the jet stream from Houston to San Francisco.

47.
(1) The data presented in the graph does not support this conclusion. The test takers might select this alternative since mold growth in sugar water is shown in the graph. They may assume that the mold will not grow without sugar water.
(2) The data presented in the graph does not support this conclusion. The mold growth on bread with sugar water is more than the growth with salt, and this might look attractive to the test takers. However, the salt water does not seem to inhibit or slow the mold growth.
(3) The data presented in the graph does not support this conclusion. The graph shows data from mold growth only on bread. The test takers might select this alternative if they assume bread is the only medium on which mold grows well.
(4) The data presented in the graph does not support this conclusion. The test takers might select this alternative if they fail to understand the information given in the graph.
(5) **This is the correct answer. Dry bread does not show any mold growth. Molds require moisture to grow.**

48.
(1) There are places on Earth where four distinct seasons are not experienced. The test taker might select this alternative if they assume seasons are caused by the rotation of Earth on its axis.
(2) The test taker might select this alternative if they did not comprehend the information given in the stimulus. A leap year occurs every four years to help synchronize the calendar year with the solar year, or the length of time it takes the earth to complete its orbit around the sun, which is about 365¼ days. In a leap year, the extra day is added to the end of February, giving it 29 days instead of the usual 28 days. However, Earth completing one turn in 24 hours does not explain leap year.
(3) This is the correct answer. Earth rotates from west to east in 24 hours, and the sun appears to rise in the east.
(4) The test taker might select this alternative since this is a correct statement. However, the information given pertains to the rising of the sun in the east.
(5) The test taker might select this alternative if they did not comprehend the information given in the stimulus. The stimulus does not explain the latitudes.

49.
(1) The test takers might select this alternative if they do not understand the information given in the Punnett Square. To be pure for the tall gene, each parent needs to carry two dominant tallness genes (TT). Based on the Punnett Square, both parents were hybrids.
(2) The test takers might select this alternative if they do not understand the information given in the Punnett Square. To be pure for the short gene, each parent needs to carry two recessive shortness genes (tt). Based on the Punnett Square, both parents were hybrids.
(3) The test takers might select this alternative if they do not understand the information given in the Punnett Square. Based on the Punnett Square, both parents were hybrids. They contained one dominant tallness gene and one recessive shortness gene (Tt).
(4) This is the correct answer. Both parents carry one dominant tallness gene and one recessive shortness gene.
(5) The test takers might select this alternative if they do not understand the information given in the Punnett Square. Based on the Punnett Square, both parents were hybrids. They contained one dominant tallness gene and one recessive shortness gene (Tt).

50.
(1) The test takers might select this alternative if they fail to compare the growth patterns illustrated in the graph. Based on the graph, in mixed culture, the paramecium population declined over time.
(2) This is the correct answer. Based on the data in the graph, this species of paramecia reproduces very poorly when grown with other species.
(3) The test takers might select this alternative if they fail to identify the growth pattern shown by the paramecium when grown alone. Based on the data from the graph, when grown alone, the paramecium population flourished over time.
(4) The test takers might select this alternative if they are unable to compare the patterns illustrated in the graph. The graph shows two different patterns of reproduction and growth when grown alone and when grown in a mixed culture with other species.
(5) The test takers might select this alternative if they make a generalization from the information given. However, there is not sufficient data and information to reach this conclusion. The graph shows the growth pattern of one species of paramecia when grown alone and when grown in mixed culture. A generalization cannot be made from this data about all other species.

Mathematics, Part I

*Exclusively provided and written by the GED Testing Service, answer explanations (rationales) for each test question are provided here for the Full-Length Official GED Practice Test.

1.
  (1) This distractor is the number of ducks counted when 1 bushel of food was available and is far below any value that would be associated with 6 bushels of food based on the pattern shown in the graph.
  (2) This distractor is the number of ducks counted when 3 bushels of food were available and is well below any value that would be associated with 6 bushels of food based on the pattern shown in the graph.
  (3) This is the correct answer. A very close approximation for the line of best fit (which test takers are not expected to generate) would be $y = 6.5x + 9$, but any reasonable sketch of a line of best fit shows that this is the only alternative even remotely close to the point on such a line when 6 bushels of food were available.
  (4) This distractor is the number of ducks counted when 9.5 bushels of food were available and is well above any values in the vicinity of 6 bushels.
  (5) This distractor is the number of ducks counted when 12 bushels of food were available and is far above any values in the vicinity of 6 bushels.

2.
  (1) This distractor is a relationship indicated by a line falling from left to right.
  (2) This distractor is a restatement of alternative (1).
  (3) This distractor is a relationship indicated by a horizontal line.
  (4) This is the correct answer. The general trend of the points is upward from left to right, and any reasonable sketch of a line of best fit would indicate that a strong, positive relationship between the variables exists.
  (5) This distractor is a condition in which a general scattering occurred and no general trend was apparent.

3.
  The correct answer is 750: $110 \times 30 + 450 - 3000 = 750$.

4.
  The correct answer is 26: $6.5 \div 0.25 = 26$.

5.
  (1) This distractor is the difference between the numbers of hours and minutes in the stem.
  (2) This distractor incorrectly subtracts times as hours and minutes (does not borrow one from the hours).
  (3) This is the correct answer: the time between 9:15 PM and midnight is 2 hours and 45 minutes; the time between midnight and 4:45 AM is 4 hours and 45 minutes; the total time is 6 hours and 90 minutes, or 7 hours and 30 minutes, which is 7.5 hours.
  (4) This distractor incorrectly computes the time from 9:15 PM to midnight as 3 hours 45 minutes (does not borrow one from the hours).
  (5) This distractor is the sum of the times as hours and minutes.

6.
  (1) This is the correct answer: $100\% - (65\% + 18\% + 10\% + 4\%) = 3\%$.
  (2) This distractor is the percent of nitrogen.
  (3) This distractor is the percent of hydrogen.
  (4) This distractor is the percent of carbon.
  (5) This distractor is the percent of oxygen.

7.
  (1) This distractor is the number of kilograms of elements other than those in the chart.
  (2) This distractor is the number of kilograms of nitrogen.
  (3) This distractor is the number of kilograms of hydrogen.
  (4) This distractor is the number of kilograms of carbon.
  (5) This is the correct answer: $80 \times 0.65 = 52$.

8.
  (1) This distractor is the number of karats.
  (2) This distractor is the denominator.
  (3) This distractor would be selected if a person used the expression $24 + 18 + 1$ (numbers in the stem) as a percent or $\frac{(18 - 1 - 5)}{28}$ (miskey).
  (4) This is the correct answer: $\frac{18}{24} = 0.75$, or 75%.
  (5) This distractor is the result of dividing inversely $\left(\frac{24}{18}\right)$.

9.
  (1) This distractor is the result of the following miskeys: $(6.0 + 10) \div (60 \div 10)$.
  (2) This distractor is the result of the following miskeys: $(60 + 6.0) \div (6.0 + 11)$.
  (3) This distractor is the result of the following miskeys and selected as the only distractor close to the rounded answer: $(10 \times 10) \div (6.0 + 10)$.
  (4) This distractor is the result of the following miskeys: $(50 \times 10) \div (60 + 10)$.
  (5) This is the correct answer: $(60 \times 10) \div (60 + 10) = \frac{600}{70} \approx 8.57$.

10.
  The correct answer is $\frac{9}{16}$, or .5625. When the given fractions are expressed using their least common denominator, the pattern emerges. The least common denominator for 8, 16, and 2 is 16. $\frac{3}{8} = \frac{6}{16}; \frac{1}{2} = \frac{8}{16}; \frac{5}{8} = \frac{10}{16}$. The ordered set of values becomes $\frac{6}{16}, \frac{7}{16}, \frac{8}{16}, x, \frac{10}{16}$. The pattern shows that the value of x is $\frac{9}{16}$, which could also be expressed as its decimal equivalent.

11.
  (1) This distractor has a faster speed/slope (5.0).
  (2) This is the correct answer: the distance (y-intercept: 20) is greater, and the speed/slope is the same (4.5).
  (3) This distractor has a slower speed/slope (2.5).
  (4) This distractor has a lesser distance (y-intercept: 10) and a faster speed/slope (5.0).
  (5) This distractor has a lesser distance (y-intercept: 10).

12.
  (1) This is the correct answer: the distance/y-intercept is greater (12), and the speed/slope is less (not as steep).
  (2) This distractor suggests that the distances/y-intercepts are the same, which they are not.
  (3) This distractor suggests that the distance/y-intercept is less, but it is greater.
  (4) This distractor suggests that the speed/slope is greater (steeper), but it is less.

(5) This distractor suggests that the distance/y-intercept is less when it is greater and the speed/slope is greater (steeper) when it is less.

13.
(1) This distractor is the radius from a miscalculated diameter.
(2) This is the correct answer. The width of the rectangle is the diameter of one circle, and the height of the rectangle is two diameters. $(2d)(d) = 50; 2d^2 = 50; d^2 = 25; d = \sqrt{25}; d = 5$. If the diameter is 5, the radius is 2.5.
(3) This distractor is the diameter miscalculated.
(4) This distractor is the diameter.
(5) This distractor is the sum of a diameter and a radius.

14.
(1) This distractor is an incorrect day.
(2) This is the correct answer: $78 + 86 + 97 + 59 = 320$, which is less than the sum of pizzas sold on any other day.
(3) This distractor is an incorrect day.
(4) This distractor is an incorrect day.
(5) This distractor is an incorrect day.

15.
(1) This distractor is the minimum number sold at Store C.
(2) This distractor is the number sold at Store D on Thursday.
(3) This distractor is the number sold at Store C on Monday.
(4) This is the correct answer: $(114 + 97 + 111 + 125 + 158) \div 5 = 121$.
(5) This distractor is the mean for Store B.

16.
The correct answer is 218: $146 + 189 + 158 + 142 − (95 + 120 + 114 + 88) = 218$.

17.
The correct answer is 13.50, or 13.5: $1.5 \times 7 + 3 = 13.5$.

18.
(1) This distractor does not include 200 added to the total collected.
(2) This distractor is the sum of 350 and 200.
(3) This is the correct answer: $150 \times 30 + 200 − 4000 = 700$.
(4) This distractor results from the following miscalculation: $130 \times 50 + 200 − 4000$.
(5) This distractor results from the following miscalculation: $20 \times 150 + 300$.

19.
(1) This distractor is the result of a subtraction error or miskey (subtracted 5.95 instead of 4.95).
(2) This the correct answer: $3.25 + 2.25 + 1.25 − 4.95$.
(3) This distractor is the result of a subtraction error or miskey (subtracted 3.95 instead of 4.95).
(4) This distractor is the cost of the special.
(5) This distractor is the result of not subtracting the cost of the special.

20.
(1) This distractor is the result of using only one of each item ordered.
(2) This distractor is the result of using only 1 bowl of soup and only 1 coffee.
(3) This distractor is the result of using only 1 bowl of soup.
(4) This is the correct answer: $2 \times 4.20 + 3.75 + 2 \times 2.25 + 2.35 + 3 \times 1.25$.
(5) This distractor is the result of using 2 chicken sandwiches and 2 salads.

21.
(1) This distractor is the tax on the items purchased.
(2) This distractor is the cost of the three items purchased.
(3) This distractor is the total cost of the order with tax.
(4) This is the correct answer: $20 − (4.75 + 1.50 + 1.25) − 0.06 \times (4.75 + 1.50 + 1.25) = 12.05$.
(5) This distractor is the result of not adding the tax before subtracting.

22.
(1) This distractor is the number of items on the menu.
(2) This distractor is the number of sandwiches multiplied by the number of drinks.
(3) This distractor is the number of sandwiches multiplied by the sum of the numbers of side orders and drinks.
(4) This distractor is the result of 3 incorrectly used as the number of drinks.
(5) This is the correct answer: $4 \times 3 \times 4$.

23.
The correct answer is 840. $1200 \times 0.70 = 840$.

24.
(1) This distractor is $(10 + \sqrt{5}) \div 2$.
(2) This distractor is $[10 + (1 + \sqrt{5})] \div 2$.
(3) This distractor is $(10 \times \sqrt{5}) \div 2$.
(4) This distractor is $[10 \times \sqrt{(1 + 5)}] \div 2$.
(5) This is the correct answer: $[10 \times (1 + \sqrt{5})] \div 2 \approx 16.2$.

25.
(1) This distractor is one-quarter of the circumference if the radius rather than the diameter is used in the circumference formula.
(2) This distractor is the radius of the circular path.
(3) This is the correct answer. The path shown is one-quarter of the circumference: $\frac{1}{4} \times 3.14 \times 10 \approx 7.9$.
(4) This distractor is the incorrect circumference if the radius rather than the diameter is used in the circumference formula.
(5) This distractor is the entire circumference rather than only one-quarter.

26.
(1) This is the correct answer: $120 + 160 − \sqrt{(120^2 + 160^2)} = 80$.
(2) This distractor is the distance along Harbor Street.
(3) This distractor is the distance through Cates Park.
(4) This distractor is the sum of the distances along the streets.
(5) This distractor is the sum of the distances along the streets increased by half the distance through Cates Park.

Mathematics, Part II

*Exclusively provided and written by the GED Testing Service, answer explanations (rationales) for each test question are provided here for the Full-Length Official GED Practice Test.

27.
 (1) This distractor has arrival and departure times that are the same.
 (2) This distractor has arrival and departure times that are the same.
 (3) This distractor has arrival and departure times that are the same.
 (4) This is the correct answer: the bus arrives in Fayetteville at 11:50 AM and departs at 12:50 PM, which is one hour later.
 (5) This distractor has arrival and departure times that are the same.

28.
 (1) This distractor has a longer travel time (45 minutes).
 (2) This distractor has a longer travel time (35 minutes).
 (3) This is the correct answer: the travel time is the shortest (30 minutes); if the speed remains constant, the distance would be the least.
 (4) This distractor has a longer travel time (35 minutes).
 (5) This distractor has a longer travel time (45 minutes).

29.
 (1) This distractor is only 20 minutes later.
 (2) This distractor is only 30 minutes later.
 (3) This distractor is only 1 hour later.
 (4) This distractor is 1 hour and 10 minutes later.
 (5) This is the correct answer: 1:45 PM + 1 hour and 20 minutes would be 3:05 PM.

30.
 (1) This distractor results from dividing 160 by 4.
 (2) This is the correct answer: 260 ÷ 4 = 65.
 (3) This distractor is the result of a computation error or using the wrong number of returns.
 (4) This distractor is the number of returns without errors when the same miscalculation in alternative (3) is used.
 (5) This distractor is the number of returns without errors.

31.
 The correct answer is 7: 835 − 275 = 560; 560 ÷ 80 = 7.

32.
 (1) This distractor misinterprets the point of intersection as 80, which is then divided by 2 (the number of companies).
 (2) This distractor misreads or rounds the initial charge for Able Rentals.
 (3) This distractor is the initial charge for Banner Trucks.
 (4) This distractor misinterprets the point of intersection.
 (5) This is the correct answer: the point of intersection where the charges are the same is 100 miles.

33.
 (1) This distractor is an estimate based on interpreting $80 as $75.
 (2) This distractor is an incorrect estimate of the value, which is much closer to $80 than $70.
 (3) This is the correct answer. The value is much closer to $80.
 (4) This distractor rounds the value to the nearest value on the vertical scale.
 (5) This distractor is the charge at Able Rentals for driving 180 km.

34.
 (1) This distractor is the sum of the charges from Able Rentals and Banner Trucks.
 (2) This distractor is the charge at Banner Trucks.
 (3) This distractor is the charge at Able Rentals.
 (4) This is the correct answer: $60 - $45 - $15.
 (5) This distractor assumes that there is no charge since the truck was not used.

35.
 The correct answer is the point (1, -4). When a shape is moved by a translation, all points follow the same movement pattern. Moving the point (4, 1) using the same movement pattern described in the stem, {3 left, 5 down}, would move the point to the new location of (1, -4). Translation patterns can also be thought of as arithmetic operations. Moving left or down is equivalent to subtracting; moving right or up is equivalent to adding. If 3 and 5 are subtracted from their respective coordinates, the result would be (4 − 3, 1 − 5), which would be the point (1, -4).

36.
 (1) This distractor is the percent.
 (2) This distractor is 350 multiplied by 10% rather than 20%.
 (3) This is the correct answer: 350 × 0.20 = 70.
 (4) This distractor is the number of employees not eligible.
 (5) This distractor is the difference between numbers in the stem (350 − 20).

37.
 (1) This is the correct answer: 180 − (36 + 36).
 (2) This distractor interprets the angle shown to be a right angle.
 (3) This distractor is the sum of angles P and S.
 (4) This distractor is the given measure of angle P.
 (5) This distractor assumes that the measure of angle S is unknown. Angles P and S are opposite sides RS and RP, respectively, which are radii of the circle and therefore equal. In any triangle, angles opposite equal sides have equal measures. Therefore, angle P and angle S both measure 36 degrees.

38.
 (1) This distractor assumes that all will increase.
 (2) This is the correct answer. When all values in a data set are increased or decreased by the same number, the standard deviation does not change. The mean and the median increase (by 5) because all numbers are larger. This also can be seen on a graph. If the original ages were plotted and compared to the plot of all ages increased by 5, the shape of the plots would be exactly the same. Standard deviation is one of two measures of dispersion (the other being range) with which GED candidates should be familiar. Two graphs on the same scale that have the same shape have the same standard deviation (and range).

- (3) This distractor only correctly recognizes that the mean increases by 5.
- (4) This distractor only correctly recognizes that the median increases by 5.
- (5) This distractor assumes that the changes for the mean and median are the result of the product of the number of people in the group (100) and the number of years (5) and that the standard deviation will increase when, in fact, it will not.

39.
- **(1) This is the correct answer: $0.02 × 20 + $0.01 × 40 + $0.05 × 30 = $2.30.**
- (2) This distractor is calculated using only 40 cans and 20 plastic bottles.
- (3) This distractor is calculated using only 40 cans.
- (4) This distractor is calculated using only 40 glass containers.
- (5) This distractor is the total number of items (90) times the total of all reimbursements ($0.08).

40.
- (1) This distractor uses the same number of glass containers (x).
- (2) This distractor uses $2x$ to represent the number of all items rather than only the number of glass containers.
- **(3) This is the correct answer: the number of cans and plastic bottles are both represented by x, and the number of glass containers is twice as great ($2x$).**
- (4) This distractor uses the sum of the reimbursements multiplied by the same number of items for all (x).
- (5) This distractor uses the sum of the reimbursements multiplied by $2x$ for all items.

41.
- (1) This distractor is a computation error for the reimbursement for 1000 cans. The actual computation would yield $20.00.
- **(2) This is the correct answer: 1000 × $0.02 = $20; $20 ÷ $0.05 = 400.**
- (3) This distractor is computed from 1000 − (1000 × 0.01) ÷ 0.05.
- (4) This distractor is the number of aluminum cans.
- (5) This distractor is the number of cans divided by 0.05.

42.
- (1) This distractor is the area of the walls minus the area of the doors: 2(5 + 4) × 3 − 1 × 2.
- (2) This distractor is the volume of the room minus the perimeter of the door: 5 × 4 × 3 − 2(1 + 2).
- (3) This distractor is the volume of the room minus the area of the door: 5 × 4 × 3 − 1 × 2.
- (4) This distractor is the volume of the room: 5 × 4 × 3.
- **(5) This is the correct answer; no amount of paint needed or cost per gallon of the paint is known.**

43.
> The correct answer is 1/100, or 0.01. Probability is the number of successes (1 red ball) divided by the number of possible outcomes (100 balls).

44.
- (1) This distractor is the sum of the cost of one of each stamp.
- (2) This distractor is the cost of 7 21-cent stamps.
- **(3) This is the correct answer: $0.34 + 6 × $0.21.**
- (4) This distractor is the cost of one 21-cent stamp and 6 34-cent stamps.
- (5) This distractor is the cost of 7 34-cent stamps.

45.
- (1) This distractor is only 20 minutes later.
- (2) This distractor is only 40 minutes later.
- (3) This distractor is 1 hour and 20 minutes later.
- **(4) This is the correct answer: 1 hour after 9:55 AM, it is 10:55 AM; 40 minutes later, it is 11:35 AM.**
- (5) This distractor is 2 hours and 40 minutes later.

46.
- **(1) This is the correct answer. The magenta line representing the actual cost should be used.**
- (2) This distractor is the approximate actual cost of driving 2500 km.
- (3) This distractor is the difference between reimbursement and actual cost for driving 2000 km.
- (4) This distractor is the difference between reimbursement and actual cost for driving 2500 km.
- (5) This distractor is the reimbursement for driving 2000 km.

47.
> The correct answer is (0, 4). When the segment is rotated as described, the new location of point F will be (-5, 4). The coordinates of the midpoint of the segment with endpoints (5, 4) (point D) and (-5, 4) (the new location of point F) are the averages of the coordinates of the endpoints: (-5 + 5)/2 and (4 + 4)/2, which are 0/2, or 0, and 8/4, or 4.

48.
- (1) This distractor is the number of minutes.
- (2) This distractor is the number of liters pumped by a large pump in 4 minutes.
- (3) This distractor is the number of liters pumped by a large pump in 5 minutes.
- (4) This distractor is the number of liters pumped in 6 minutes by the large pump only.
- **(5) This is the correct answer: 12 + 3 = 15.**

49.
- (1) This distractor is the number of liters pumped by a small pump in 4 minutes.
- **(2) This is the correct answer: 8 − 2 = 6.**
- (3) This distractor is the number of liters pumped by a large pump in 4 minutes.
- (4) This distractor is the sum rather than the difference.
- (5) This distractor is the average of the difference multiplied by the time.

50.
- (1) This distractor is the measure of angle A or C or assuming that $2x + 2x + x$ equals $4x$ instead of $5x$.
- (2) This distractor is the result of using 160 as the sum of the angles instead of 180.
- (3) This distractor is the result of subtracting 20 from both sides of the correct equation rather than adding 20 ($5x − 20 = 180$; $5x = 160$).
- **(4) This is the correct answer: $5x − 20 = 180$; $5x = 200$; $x = 40$; angle B = $2x = 2(40) = 80$.**
- (5) This distractor is the result of using 200 as the sum of the angles rather than 180.

Essay Directions and Topic E

This page includes background information for the Full-Length Test Form E topic and directions for the Language Arts, Writing Test, Part II. *Essays written by graduating high school seniors and scored by the GED Writing Committee and the Committee's scores and commentaries can be found on pages VI-I-U.S.-PE-1–30 of the Official GED Practice Tests Administrator's Manual, which contains information for all the half-length Tests, PA–PG.*

Look at the box on page 63. In the box is your assigned topic and the letter of that topic.

You must write on the assigned topic ONLY.

Mark the letter of your assigned topic in the appropriate space on your answer sheet booklet. Be certain that all other requested information is properly recorded in your answer sheet booklet.

You will have 45 minutes to write on your assigned essay topic. If you have time remaining in this test period after you complete your essay, you may return to the multiple-choice section. Do not return the *Language Arts, Writing Test* booklet to your examiner until you finish both *Parts I* and *II* of the *Language Arts, Writing Test*.

Two evaluators will score your essay according to its overall effectiveness. Their scores will be based on the following features:

- well-focused main points
- clear organization
- specific development of your ideas
- control of sentence structure, punctuation, grammar, word choice, and spelling

REMEMBER, YOU MUST COMPLETE BOTH THE MULTIPLE-CHOICE QUESTIONS (*PART I*) AND THE ESSAY (*PART II*) TO RECEIVE A SCORE ON THE *LANGUAGE ARTS, WRITING TEST*.

To avoid having to repeat both parts of the test, be sure to do the following:

- Do not leave the pages blank.
- Write legibly in ink so that the evaluators will be able to read your writing.
- Write on the assigned topic. If you write on a topic other than the one assigned, you will not receive a score for the *Language Arts, Writing Test*.
- Write your essay on the lined pages of the separate answer sheet booklet. Only the writing on these pages will be scored.

IMPORTANT:
The essay that you write is the property of the GED Testing Service (GEDTS) and is considered confidential and secure. GEDTS policy prohibits the return of the essay to you, your family, or any other individual or program. The policy further prohibits you from discussing or publicizing the content of your essay.

TOPIC E

We all have different views of what it means to be a successful person.

In your essay, identify someone whom you consider successful. Explain what qualities make that person a "success" in your view. Use your personal observations, experience, and knowledge to support your essay.

Part II is a test to determine how well you can use written language to explain your ideas.

In preparing your essay, you should take the following steps:
- Read the **DIRECTIONS** and the **TOPIC** carefully.
- Plan your essay before you write. Use the scratch paper provided to make any notes. These notes will be collected but not scored.
- Before you turn in your essay, reread what you have written and make any changes that will improve your essay.

Your essay should be long enough to develop the topic adequately.

Scoring the Essay

Readers use the following GED Testing Service approved scoring guide:
- 4 = Effective—reader understands and easily follows the writer's expression of ideas,
- 3 = Adequate—reader understands the writer's ideas,
- 2 = Marginal—reader occasionally has difficulty understanding or following the writer's ideas, and
- 1 = Inadequate—reader has difficulty identifying or following the writer's ideas.

Readers use the following five major descriptors in grading and in writing commentary for each essay:
- Response to the Prompt,
- Organization,
- Development and Details,
- Conventions of Edited American English, and
- Word Choice

	1 Inadequate	2 Marginal	3 Adequate	4 Effective
	Reader has difficulty identifying or following the writer's ideas.	Reader occasionally has difficulty understanding or following the writer's ideas.	Reader understands writer's ideas.	Reader understands and easily follows the writer's expression of ideas.
Response to the Prompt	Attempts to address prompt but with little or no success in establishing a focus.	Addresses the prompt, though the focus may shift.	Uses the writing prompt to establish a main idea.	Presents a clearly focused main idea that addresses the prompt.
Organization	Fails to organize ideas.	Shows some evidence of an organizational plan.	Uses an identifiable organizational plan.	Establishes a clear and logical organization.
Development and Details	Demonstrates little or no development; usually lacks details or examples or presents irrelevant information.	Has some development but lacks specific details; may be llimited to a listing, repetitions, or generalizations.	Has focused but occasionally uneven development; incorporates some specific detail.	Achieves coherent development with specific and relevant details and examples.
Conventions of EAE	May exhibit minimal or no control of sentence structure and the conventions of EAE.	May demonstrate inconsistent control of sentence structure and the conventions of EAE.	Generally controls sentence structure and the conventions of EAE.	Consistently controls sentence structure and the conventions of Edited American English (EAE).
Word Choice	Exhibits weak and/or inappropriate words.	Exhibits a narrow range of word choice, often including inappropriate selections.	Exhibits appropriate word choice.	Exhibits varied and precise word choice.

© 2008, American Council on Education/The GED Testing Service

Official GED Practice Tests Administrator's Guide: Full-Length Test Form

Essay Tips

The tips that follow will help you write an effective GED essay. You do not need any specialized knowledge to write a good essay. Use your own opinions and experience to write your views on a topic. Follow these steps to write an effective essay.

Plan Your Essay

- Take time to understand the writing assignment (also called a writing prompt or topic).
- Reread the assignment several times to make sure you understand what is being asked. Look for words like *causes, reasons, effects, advantages, similarities,* or *opinions.* These words will help you formulate what you should write.
- Think about the most important point you want to express in your essay. This is your main idea. Write down a few ideas about the topic on scratch paper. There is no right answer, but as you write ideas, make sure they are broad enough to cover all of your supporting examples.
- Think of a few examples to support the assignment using your main idea as the focus. Write down thoughts or ideas about your main idea on the topic.

Organize Your Essay

- If you have similar examples or ideas, group them together. Each group will later become a paragraph in your essay.
- Then expand the groups with additional thoughts or examples. You may find that thinking of experiences you or your friends have had will help you add to your list.
- Order your groups in a logical flow. You can arrange your groups in order of importance or in a way that would allow you to compare one group (paragraph) to another. Putting your ideas into an outline may help you write your essay.

How to Raise the Essay Score

The following paragraphs describe possible problems in your essay. These problems lower your essay score considerably. Use the suggestions in the paragraphs to revise your essay. Revising your essay may raise the score the next time it's scored. As you are revising your essay, remember you are trying to write an essay that convinces your reader you understand and can address the topic. Show the reader you have an opinion about the topic that you can support in your essay using good writing.

Response to the Prompt: Although you may have tried to address the topic you were assigned, your essay has little or no focus. This makes the ideas in your essay difficult to understand. Each essay prompt provides a topic or question about which your essay must be written. Read and think about the question or topic until you are sure you know your opinion about the essay topic or question. Then decide on a main idea that you can develop with supporting points.

Organization: To organize your essay, make a plan before beginning to write or rewrite. Create an outline that shows the main idea and the supporting ideas. Organize your thoughts into paragraphs that provide a logical ordering of your ideas. Be sure each paragraph discusses one idea that supports the main idea or topic sentence of your essay. This will help you organize an essay with ideas that are easy to identify and follow.

Development and Details: Although you may have fully developed one or more ideas, you have not developed all of your ideas or provided enough detail to illustrate your points. Your plan should include two to four points that support the main idea of your essay. Explain each of these supporting points in a separate paragraph with one or more facts, details, or specific examples.

Sentence Structure and Edited American English: Your essay needs a better variety of sentence structure and needs to closely follow the rules of good grammar (Edited American English). Grammatically correct sentences that vary in sentence structure are easy to read and understand. Make sure each of your sentences contains a subject and a verb. Each sentence should begin with a capital letter and end with an appropriate punctuation mark. Be clear about where one thought stops and the next begins. Make sure that sentences do not join two unrelated thoughts. Finally, check your work for misspelled words and proper punctuation.

Word Choice: Some of the words you use in your essay are inappropriate for your writing task. They may be vague, weak, or inappropriate. Misusing words that sound the same, using words whose meanings you do not understand, or omitting words and letters make your essay difficult to read. When you write, choose your words carefully and use them in their correct forms and parts of speech. The words you choose and the way you use them should help to make your meaning clearer. If you used slang or profanity, eliminate it now.

> For additional information on grading GED essays as well as examples of scored essays, please refer to the Official GED Practice Tests Administrator's Manual, which contains information for all the half-length Official GED Practice Tests, PA–PG.

66 *Official GED Practice Tests Administrator's Guide: Full-Length Test Form*

Steck-Vaughn Recommended Prescriptions for Additional Study

Language Arts, Writing

Study material for the 2002 Series GED® Tests

Sentence Structure

STECK-VAUGHN GED Language Arts, Writing © 2002, pp. 34–39, 42–47, 54–59, 62–67, 72–75, 78–81

STECK-VAUGHN GED Writing Exercise Book © 2002, pp. 4–19

STECK-VAUGHN Complete GED Preparation © 2002, pp. 68–89

STECK-VAUGHN PreGED Writing © 2000, pp. 31, 40–45, 50, 53–55, 62–63, 129, 187–201, 212–219

STECK-VAUGHN GED 21st Century Software © 2003, Sentence Structure Skill Builder

STECK-VAUGHN PreGED Writing © 2003, pp. 168–183

Usage

STECK-VAUGHN GED Language Arts, Writing © 2002, pp. 136–143, 148–153, 158–163, 168–175

STECK-VAUGHN GED Writing Exercise Book © 2002, pp. 34–48

STECK-VAUGHN Complete GED Preparation © 2002, pp. 114–127

STECK-VAUGHN PreGED Writing © 2000, pp. 28, 30, 38–39, 51–52, 66–67, 102–103, 116–117, 127–128, 140, 169–186, 212–219

STECK-VAUGHN GED 21st Century Software © 2003, Usage Skill Builder

STECK-VAUGHN PreGED Writing © 2003, pp. 150–167

Mechanics

STECK-VAUGHN GED Language Arts, Writing © 2002, pp. 188–193, 196–201, 208–215

STECK-VAUGHN GED Writing Exercise Book © 2002, pp. 49–60

STECK-VAUGHN Complete GED Preparation © 2002, pp. 132–141

STECK-VAUGHN PreGED Writing © 2000, pp. 87–89, 118, 156–168, 212–219

STECK-VAUGHN GED 21st Century Software © 2003, Mechanics Skill Builder

STECK-VAUGHN PreGED Writing © 2003, pp. 184–197

Organization

STECK-VAUGHN GED Language Arts, Writing © 2002, pp. 94–99, 104–107, 112–115, 120–123

STECK-VAUGHN GED Writing Exercise Book © 2002, pp. 20–33

STECK-VAUGHN Complete GED Preparation © 2002, pp. 96–108

STECK-VAUGHN PreGED Writing © 2000, pp. 14–25, 27, 32–33, 56, 64–65, 68–69, 90–91, 125–126, 130–131, 138–139, 142–143, 212–219

STECK-VAUGHN GED 21st Century Software © 2003, Organization Skill Builder

STECK-VAUGHN PreGED Writing © 2003, pp. 198–207

Steck-Vaughn Recommended Prescriptions for Additional Study

Language Arts, Writing Essay

STECK-VAUGHN GED Essay © 2002, pp. 16–23, 28–37, 42–55, 60–75, 80–87, 92–97, 102–107

STECK-VAUGHN GED Language Arts, Writing Exercise Book © 2002, pp. 20–33, 74–75, 90–91

STECK-VAUGHN Complete GED Preparation © 2002, pp. 158–198

STECK-VAUGHN PreGED Writing © 2000, pp. 14–17, 124–145, 156–201, 212–219

STECK-VAUGHN GED 21st Century Software © 2003, Topic 1 Skill Builder, Topic 2 Skill Builder, Topic 3 Skill Builder, Topic 4 Skill Builder

Language Arts, Reading

Study material for the 2002 Series GED® Tests

Poetry

STECK-VAUGHN GED Language Arts, Reading © 2002, pp. 170–173, 176–179, 182–185, 188–191, 194–197

STECK-VAUGHN GED Reading Exercise Book © 2002, pp. 44–53

STECK-VAUGHN Complete GED Preparation © 2002, pp. 422–435

STECK-VAUGHN PreGED Reading © 2000, pp. 146–149, 152–155

STECK-VAUGHN GED 21st Century Software © 2003, Poetry Skill Builder

STECK-VAUGHN PreGED Reading © 2003, pp. 186–213

Drama

STECK-VAUGHN GED Language Arts, Reading © 2002, pp. 210–213, 216–219, 222–225, 228–231

STECK-VAUGHN GED Reading Exercise Book © 2002, pp. 54–63

STECK-VAUGHN Complete GED Preparation © 2002, pp. 438–447

STECK-VAUGHN PreGED Reading © 2000, pp. 134–137, 140–143

STECK-VAUGHN GED 21st Century Software © 2003, Drama Skill Builder

STECK-VAUGHN PreGED Reading © 2003, pp. 158–184

Fiction

STECK-VAUGHN GED Language Arts, Reading © 2002, pp. 100–103, 106–109, 112–115, 118–121, 124–127, 130–133, 136–139, 142–145, 148–151, 154–157

STECK-VAUGHN GED Reading Exercise Book © 2002, pp. 19–43

STECK-VAUGHN Complete GED Preparation © 2002, pp. 392–419

STECK-VAUGHN PreGED Reading © 2000, pp. 14–17, 20–23, 26–29, 32–35, 38–41, 44–47, 50–53

STECK-VAUGHN GED 21st Century Software © 2003, Fiction Skill Builder

STECK-VAUGHN PreGED Reading © 2003, pp. 98–156

General Nonfiction

STECK-VAUGHN GED Language Arts, Reading © 2002, pp. 34–39, 42–45, 48–51, 54–57, 60–63, 66–69, 72–75, 78–81, 84–87

STECK-VAUGHN GED Language Arts, Reading Exercise Book © 2002, pp. 4–18

STECK-VAUGHN Complete GED Preparation © 2002, pp. 366–389

Steck-Vaughn Recommended Prescriptions for Additional Study

Language Arts, Reading (continued)

STECK-VAUGHN PreGED Reading © 2000, pp. 68–71, 74–77, 80–83, 86–89, 92–95, 98–101, 104–107, 110–113, 116–119

STECK-VAUGHN GED 21st Century Software © 2003, General Nonfiction Skill Builder

Reviews of Visual Arts

STECK-VAUGHN GED Language Arts, Reading © 2002, pp. 86–87

STECK-VAUGHN GED Language Arts, Reading Exercise Book © 2002, pp. 9–13

STECK-VAUGHN Complete GED Preparation © 2002, pp. 389, 390–391

STECK-VAUGHN PreGED Reading © 2000, pp. 110–113

STECK-VAUGHN GED 21st Century Software © 2003, Workplace and Community Documents Skill Builder

Workplace and Community Documents

STECK-VAUGHN GED Language Arts, Reading © 2002, pp. 44–47, 51–57

STECK-VAUGHN GED Reading Exercise Book © 2002, pp. 14–18

STECK-VAUGHN Complete GED Preparation © 2002, pp. 370, 373–374, 376

STECK-VAUGHN PreGED Reading © 2000, pp. 168–171, 174–177, 180–183, 186–189, 192–195, 198–203

STECK-VAUGHN GED 21st Century Software © 2003, Workplace and Community Documents Skill Builder

STECK-VAUGHN PreGED Reading © 2003, pp. 22–39

Steck-Vaughn Recommended Prescriptions for Additional Study

Social Studies

Study material for the 2002 Series GED₀ Tests

U.S. History

STECK-VAUGHN GED Social Studies © 2002, pp. 34–39, 42-47, 50-55, 58-63, 66-71, 74-81
STECK-VAUGHN GED Social Studies Exercise Book © 2002, pp. 4–15
STECK-VAUGHN Complete GED Preparation © 2002, pp. 202–220
STECK-VAUGHN PreGED Social Studies © 2000, pp. 88–91, 94–97, 100–103, 106–109, 112–115, 118–121, 124–127
STECK-VAUGHN GED 21st Century Software © 2003, U.S. History Skill Builder
STECK-VAUGHN PreGED Social Studies © 2003, pp. 14–64

World History

STECK-VAUGHN Complete GED Preparation © 2002, pp. 224–236
STECK-VAUGHN GED 21st Century Software © 2003, World History Skill Builder
STECK-VAUGHN GED Social Studies © 2002, pp. 96–101, 104-109, 112-117, 120-125
STECK-VAUGHN GED Social Studies Exercise Book © 2002, pp. 16-23
STECK-VAUGHN PreGED Social Studies © 2000, pp. 48-51, 54-57, 60-63, 66-69, 72-75
STECK-VAUGHN PreGED Social Studies © 2003, pp. 66-104

Geography

STECK-VAUGHN GED Social Studies © 2002, pp. 210–215, 218-223, 226-231
STECK-VAUGHN GED Social Studies Exercise Book © 2002, pp. 45–55
STECK-VAUGHN Complete GED Preparation © 2002, pp. 268–277
STECK-VAUGHN PreGED Social Studies © 2000, pp. 14–17, 20–23, 26–29, 32–35
STECK-VAUGHN GED 21st Century Software © 2003, Geography Skill Builder

Economics

STECK-VAUGHN GED Social Studies © 2002, pp. 178–183, 186–191, 194–199
STECK-VAUGHN GED Social Studies Exercise Book © 2002, pp. 35–44
STECK-VAUGHN Complete GED Preparation © 2002, pp. 256–264
STECK-VAUGHN PreGED Social Studies © 2000, pp. 180–183, 186–189, 192–195, 198–201, 204–207
STECK-VAUGHN GED 21st Century Software © 2003, Economics Skill Builder
STECK-VAUGHN PreGED Social Studies © 2003, pp. 146–184

Civics and Government

STECK-VAUGHN GED Social Studies © 2002, pp. 136–141, 144–149, 152–157, 160–165
STECK-VAUGHN GED Social Studies Exercise Book © 2002, pp. 24–34
STECK-VAUGHN Complete GED Preparation © 2002, pp. 240–252
STECK-VAUGHN PreGED Social Studies © 2000, pp. 140–143, 146–149, 152–155, 158–161, 164–167
STECK-VAUGHN GED 21st Century Software © 2003, Civics and Government Skill Builder
STECK-VAUGHN PreGED Social Studies © 2003, pp. 106–144

Steck-Vaughn Recommended Prescriptions for Additional Study

Science

Study material for the 2002 Series GED® Tests

Life Science

STECK-VAUGHN GED Science © 2002, pp. 36–39, 44–47, 52–55, 60–63, 68–71, 76–79, 84–87, 92–95

STECK-VAUGHN GED Science Exercise Book © 2002, pp. 4–20

STECK-VAUGHN Complete GED Preparation © 2002, pp. 290–313

STECK-VAUGHN PreGED Science © 2002, pp. 14–17, 20–23, 26–29, 32–35, 38–41, 44–47, 50–53, 56–59, 62–65, 68–71, 74–77, 80–83, 86–89, 94–99

STECK-VAUGHN GED 21st Century Software © 2003, Life Science Skill Builder

STECK-VAUGHN PreGED Science © 2003, pp. 14–100

Earth and Space Science

STECK-VAUGHN GED Science © 2002, pp. 112–115, 120–123, 128–131, 136–139, 144–147

STECK-VAUGHN GED Science Exercise Book © 2002, pp. 21–31

STECK-VAUGHN Complete GED Preparation © 2002, pp. 316-331

STECK-VAUGHN PreGED Science © 2002, pp. 104–107, 110-113, 116-119, 122-125, 128-131, 138-139

STECK-VAUGHN GED 21st Century Software © 2003, Earth and Space Science Skill Builder

STECK-VAUGHN PreGED Science © 2003, pp. 102-140

Physical Science

STECK-VAUGHN GED Science © 2002, pp. 160-163, 168-171, 176-179, 184-187, 192-195, 200-203, 208-211

STECK-VAUGHN GED Science Exercise Book © 2002, pp. 32-49

STECK-VAUGHN Complete GED Preparation © 2002, pp. 334–355

STECK-VAUGHN PreGED Science © 2002, pp. 144–147, 150–153, 156–159, 162–165, 168–171, 176–179, 184–187, 190–193, 196–199, 202–205, 210–213

STECK-VAUGHN GED 21st Century Software © 2003, Physical Science Skill Builder

STECK-VAUGHN PreGED Science © 2003, pp. 176–214

Steck-Vaughn Recommended Prescriptions for Additional Study

Mathematics

Study material for the 2002 Series GED® Tests

Number Operations and Number Sense

STECK-VAUGHN GED Mathematics © 2002, pp. 34–49, 52–65, 70–99, 104–127, 132–151

STECK-VAUGHN GED Mathematics Exercise Book © 2002, pp. 5–32, 90–94

STECK-VAUGHN Complete GED Preparation © 2002, pp. 458–530

STECK-VAUGHN PreGED Mathematics © 2000, pp. 10–19, 22–31, 34–49, 70–79, 82–93, 96–103, 116–123, 126–133, 136–145, 170–174, 242–254

STECK-VAUGHN GED 21st Century Software © 2003, Number Sense and Operations Skill Builder

STECK-VAUGHN PreGED Mathematics © 2003, pp. 12–19

Measurement and Geometry

STECK-VAUGHN GED Mathematics © 2002, pp. 164–179, 184–191, 274–293, 298–319

STECK-VAUGHN GED Mathematics Exercise Book © 2002, pp. 36–37, 74–89

STECK-VAUGHN Complete GED Preparation © 2002, pp. 536–552, 598–618

STECK-VAUGHN PreGED Mathematics © 2000, pp. 22–23, 48–49, 52–57, 90–91, 96–97, 122–123, 139, 142–143, 158–167, 170–171, 221–224, 242–254

STECK-VAUGHN GED 21st Century Software © 2003, Measurement and Geometry Skill Builder

STECK-VAUGHN PreGED Mathematics © 2003, pp. 26–27, 48–49, 56–61, 92–93, 126–127, 144–145, 168–169

Data Analysis, Statistics and Probability

STECK-VAUGHN GED Mathematics © 2002, pp. 184–197

STECK-VAUGHN GED Mathematics Exercise Book © 2002, pp. 33–35, 38–47

STECK-VAUGHN Complete GED Preparation © 2002, pp. 547–556

STECK-VAUGHN PreGED Mathematics © 2000, pp. 30–31, 46–47, 82–83, 132–133, 166–167, 182–183, 195–196, 213–220, 242–254

STECK-VAUGHN GED 21st Century Software © 2003, Data Analysis, Statistics, and Probability Skill Builder

STECK-VAUGHN PreGED Mathematics © 2003, pp. 30–31, 46–47, 90–91, 136–137, 184–185, 194–195, 206–209, 212–219

Algebra, Functions and Patterns

STECK-VAUGHN GED Mathematics © 2002, pp. 210–229, 234–261

STECK-VAUGHN GED Mathematics Exercise Book © 2002, pp. 51–73

STECK-VAUGHN Complete GED Preparation © 2002, pp. 561–593

STECK-VAUGHN PreGED Mathematics © 2000, pp. 42–43, 58–59, 130–131, 176–183, 187–196, 199–210, 242–254

STECK-VAUGHN GED 21st Century Software © 2003, Algebra, Functions and Patterns Skill Builder

STECK-VAUGHN PreGED Mathematics © 2003, pp. 17, 42–43, 54–55, 134–135, 178–183, 188–191, 198–199

For ordering information, go to www.SteckVaughn.com/GED or call 800-531-5015